Contents

FATIMA'S BOREK

Prep Time: 25 mins

Total Time: 50 mins

Servings per Recipe: 1

NUTRITIONAL VALUE

Calories 68.5 , Fat 2.2g , Cholesterol 5.6mg , Sodium 158.4mg , Carbohydrates 9.6g , Protein 2.3g

INGREDIENTS

- 20-24 spring rolls, pastry sheets
- 2 1/2-3 C. mashed potatoes
- salt
- 3/4-1 C. cheddar cheese, grated
- black pepper
- 1/2 medium brown onion, finely chopped
- flour, & water for the paste
- 1 medium pickled gherkin, finely chopped
- 3 tbsp. fresh parsley, finely chopped
- 1 tbsp. margarine or 1 tbsp. butter

DIRECTIONS

Step 1

Get a large mixing bowl: Combine in it the potato with cheese, onion, gherkin, parsley, margarine, a pinch of salt and pepper.

Step 2

Place a roll on board. Place on one side of it 2 tsp. of the filling.

Step 3

Pull one corner of the sheet over the filling and press it.

Step 4

Pull the other corner over it and coat the inside with the flour paste.

Step 5

Press it to seal it then place it aside. Repeat the process with the remaining ingredients.

Step 6

Place a large deep pan over medium heat. Heat in it 1 1/2 inch of oil.

Step 7

Cook in it the rolls until they become golden brown. Serve them warm.

Step 8

Enjoy.

ALGERIAN WEEKNIGHT DINNER (SPICY GROUND BEEF WITH BEANS)

Prep Time: 12 mins

Total Time: 28 mins

Servings per Recipe: 6

NUTRITIONAL VALUE

Calories 217.0 , Fat 8.2g , Cholesterol 49.1mg , Sodium 633.8mg , Carbohydrates 16.6g , Protein 18.4g

INGREDIENTS

- 1 lb lean ground beef

- 1 1/2 C. onions, chopped

- 1 tsp. dried basil

- 1 C. green bell pepper, chopped

- 1/2 tsp. ground black pepper

- 3 garlic cloves, crushed

- 1/4 tsp. sugar

- 8 oz. kidney beans

- 1/4 tsp. dried oregano

- 8 oz. hominy

- 1/4 tsp. red pepper flakes

- 1 tsp. salt

- 2 C. water

DIRECTIONS

Step 1

Place a large pan over medium heat. Cook in it the beef with onion, garlic and bell pepper for 7 min.

Step 2

Drain them and discard the excess grease. Pour them back into the pan.

Step 3

Add the kidney beans, hominy, salt, basil, pepper, sugar, oregano and red pepper flakes.

Step 4

Stir in 2 C. of water. Let them cook over medium heat until the stew becomes thick for at least 10 to 12 min.

Step 5

Serve it hot with some rice.

Step 6

Enjoy.

ALGERIAN QUICHE

Prep Time: 5 mins

Total Time: 1 hr 5 mins

Servings per Recipe: 10

NUTRITIONAL VALUE

Calories 174.8 , Fat 12.6g , Cholesterol 18.6mg , Sodium 719.3mg , Carbohydrates 10.7g , Protein 4.7g

INGREDIENTS

- 2 C. chickpea flour
- 1 egg, beaten
- 4 C. water
- ground cumin, for sprinkling
- 1/2 C. oil
- harissa
- 1 tbsp. salt
- 1/4 tsp. black pepper

DIRECTIONS

Step 1

Before you do anything, preheat the oven to 375 F.

Step 2

Place the flour with water, oil, salt and pepper in a blender.

Step 3

Pulse them several times until they become smooth. Pour it into a mixing bowl.

Step 4

Add to it the beaten egg and mix them well. Pour the mixture into a greased pie pan.

Step 5

Bake it for 60 min until it becomes golden brown.

Step 6

Allow the pie to cool down for few minutes then top it with the harissa.

Step 7

Serve it right away.

Step 8

Enjoy.

GROUND CHICKEN BOREK

Prep Time: 1 hr 30 mins

Total Time: 2 hr 10 mins

Servings per Recipe: 1

NUTRITIONAL VALUE

Calories 46.2 , Fat 1.3g , Cholesterol 18.3mg , Sodium 51.4mg , Carbohydrates 6.9g , Protein 1.5g

INGREDIENTS

- 36 spring roll wrappers

- 5 C. ground chicken

- 1/4 tsp. seasoning salt

- 3 large brown onions, finely chopped

- 3-4 hard-boiled eggs, finely chopped

- 1/3 C. fresh cilantro, finely chopped

- 2 tbsp. olive oil

- 1/4 preserved lemon, skin only, rinsed and

- Paste

- chopped

- 6 tbsp. plain flour

- 1/2 tsp. ras el hanout spice mix

- 1/2 C. water

DIRECTIONS

Step 1

To prepare the filling:

Step 2

Place a large saucepan over medium heat. Heat in it the oil.

Step 3

Cook in it the onion for 3 to 4 min. Stir in the chicken and cook them for 16 to 22 min while stirring.

Step 4

Stir in ras el hanout with Schwartz salt. Mix them well and cook them for 3 min.

Step 5

Stir in the chopped lemon and cook them for 2 min. Turn off the heat and fold the coriander into the mixture.

Step 6

Place the filling aside for at least 15 min to cool down completely.

Step 7

To prepare the rolls:

Step 8

Get a mixing bowl: Combine in it the flour with water until they become smooth.

Step 9

Place a sheet on a working surface. Put in it 2 tsp. of the filling.

Step 10

Pull the sides over it then roll it forward tightly.

Step 11

Brush the edge with the flour paste then press it to seal it.

Step 12

Repeat the process with the remaining ingredients.

Step 13

Place a deep pan over high heat. Heat in it about 1 1/2 inch of oil.

Step 14

Fry in it the chicken borek until they become golden brown.

Step 15

Drain them then serve them with a dip of your choice.

Step 16

Enjoy.

HOW TO MAKE HARICOT BEANS

Prep Time: 2 mins

Total Time: 2 hr 7 mins

Servings per Recipe: 6

NUTRITIONAL VALUE

Calories 107.2 , Fat 9.7g , Cholesterol 0.0mg , Sodium 984.0mg , Carbohydrates 5.4g , Protein 1.3g

INGREDIENTS

- 17.5 oz. dried haricot beans, soaked

- overnight

- 6 garlic cloves, minced

- 12 C. water

- 6-8 pieces chicken

- 6 1/2 tsp. paprika

- 4 tbsp. olive oil

- 3 1/2 tsp. ground cumin

- 1 pinch black pepper

- 14 oz. cans plum tomatoes, pureed

- 2 1/2 tsp. salt

- olive oil, & vinegar to serve

DIRECTIONS

Step 1

Place a large pot over medium heat.

Step 2

Stir in it the beans with olive oil, meat paprika, and cumin. Cook them for 4 min.

Step 3

Add to them 8 1/2 C. of water with a pinch of salt and pepper. Put on the lid and bring them to a simmer.

Step 4

Lower the heat and cook them for 60 min.

Step 5

Add 2 C. of water with tomatoes, garlic, 2 tsp. salt, 2 1/2 tsp. paprika and 1 1/2 tsp. cumin.

Step 6

Put on the lid and let them cook for 30 to 35 min.

Step 7

Once the time is up, remove the cover and let it cook for an extra 30 to 35 min.

Step 8

Stir in the vinegar with olive oil then serve them warm.

Step 9

Enjoy.

SWEET GLAZED SEMOLINA CAKE

Prep Time: 10 mins

Total Time: 50 mins

Servings per Recipe: 1

NUTRITIONAL VALUE

Calories 6699.1 , Fat 290.2g , Cholesterol 775.8mg , Sodium 1180.8mg , Carbohydrates 963.8g , Protein 83.3g

INGREDIENTS

- Cake

- 1 1/2 C. of semolina

- 4 eggs

- 1 C. plain flour

- 2 tsp. vanilla flavoring

- 2 tsp. baking powder

- Syrup

- 3/4 C. unsweetened dried shredded coconut

- 3 C. water

- 1/4 C. granulated sugar

- 3 C. granulated sugar

- 1 C. sunflower oil

- 1 tbsp. orange flower water

- 1 lemon, zest of grated

- 1 tsp. lemon juice

- 1 C. yogurt

- Garnish

- blanched whole almond

DIRECTIONS

Step 1

Before you do anything, preheat the oven to 350 F.

Step 2

To prepare the syrup:

Step 3

Place a saucepan over medium heat. Stir in it the water with sugar. Heat them until they start boiling.

Step 4

Turn off the heat. Add the orange flower water with lemon juice. Place it aside to lose heat.

Step 5

Get a large mixing bowl: Mix in it the yogurt with syrup, eggs, sunflower oil, and vanilla.

Step 6

Add the remaining dry ingredients and combine them well.

Step 7

Pour the mixture into a greased square baking pan and press it into an even layer.

Step 8

Use a knife to slice it into diamonds shapes then press an almond in the center of each diamond.

Step 9

Bake them for 32 to 42 min. Go over the diamond cuts with a knife then drizzle the syrup all over them.

Step 10

Let them sit for at least 60 min then serve them.

Step 11

Enjoy.

ALGERIAN STRAWBERRY COOKIES

Prep Time: 25 mins

Total Time: 33 mins

Servings per Recipe: 1

NUTRITIONAL VALUE

Calories 142.4 , Fat 3.9g , Cholesterol 7.4mg , Sodium 64.5mg , Carbohydrates 25.1g , Protein 1.6g

INGREDIENTS

- Cookies
- 1 tsp. baking powder
- 1 C. margarine or 1 C. butter, softened
- 1 tbsp. vanilla sugar or 1/2 tsp. vanilla extract 1/2 C. granulated sugar
- Garnish
- 1 large free range egg
- 3/4 C. strawberry jam
- 2 1/2 C. plain flour
- 1/2-3/4 C. icing sugar

DIRECTIONS

Step 1

To prepare the cookies:

Step 2

Before you do anything, preheat the oven 340 F.

Step 3

Get a large mixing bowl: Beat in it the butter with sugar until they become creamy.

Step 4

Add the vanilla with eggs and mix them well.

Step 5

Add the flour and baking powder gradually while mixing until you get a soft dough.

Step 6

Transfer the dough to a lightly floured surface and roll it until it becomes 4 mm thick.

Step 7

Use a cookie cutter to cut the dough into shapes you desire.

Step 8

Place them on a lined up baking sheet and bake them for 7 to 8 min.

Step 9

Once the time is up, turn off the oven and let them cool down for a while.

Step 10

Pull them out and place them aside to continue cooling down.

Step 11

Place a small heavy saucepan over medium heat. Pour in it the jam and heat it until it starts bubbling.

Step 12

Roll the sable cookies gently in icing sugar.

Step 13

Coat the bottom of a cookie with jam then press to it the bottom of another cookie.

Step 14

Place it on a serving plate. Repeat the process with the remaining cookies.

Step 15

Serve them right away or store them in a container for 1 week.

Step 16

Enjoy.

ALGERIAN STYLE LAMB AND BEANS

Prep Time: 20 mins

Total Time: 1 hr 35 mins

Servings per Recipe: 8

NUTRITIONAL VALUE

Calories 125.2 , Fat 2.5g , Cholesterol 68.9mg , Sodium 61.9mg , Carbohydrates 16.0g , Protein 10.4g

INGREDIENTS

- 1 lb. tripe or 1 lb. lamb, if preferred, diced 4 yellow onions, chopped
- 1 C. white beans, soaked for at least 2 hours 2-4 cloves garlic, minced
- salt
- 2 green peppers
- 4 tbsp. chopped cilantro
- 1/2 tsp. black pepper
- 2 tomatoes, chopped
- 2 tsp. cumin
- 1 tsp. paprika

DIRECTIONS

Step 1

Place the peppers on the grill and cook them until they become black.

Step 2

Transfer them to a plastic bag and seal it. Let them sit for 15 min.

Step 3

Once the time is up, peel them, rinse them and dice them.

Step 4

Place a large skillet over medium heat. Heat in it a splash of oil.

Step 5

Brown in it the lamb dices for 3 min. Place it aside.

Step 6

Add the onion with garlic, green peppers, and 3 tbsp. of olive oil.

Step 7

Stir in the seasonings and cook them for 2 min. Stir in the meat and cook them for 2 min.

Step 8

Add enough water to cover them and heat them until they start boiling.

Step 9

Bring them to a rolling boil for 60 min.

Step 10

Once the time is up, stir in the tomato and cook them for 20 min over low heat.

Step 11

Add the white beans and heat them through.

Step 12

Adjust the seasoning of your stew then serve it hot.

Step 13

Enjoy.

GREEN BEAN BOWLS

Prep Time: 10 mins

Total Time: 50 mins

Servings per Recipe: 4

NUTRITIONAL VALUE

Calories 141.0 , Fat 11.6g , Cholesterol 0.0mg , Sodium 22.0mg , Carbohydrates 8.9g , Protein 2.6g

INGREDIENTS

- 1 lb. green beans, clean and trim
- 4 C. water
- 1/4 tsp. clove, ground
- 3 tbsp. oil
- 1 tbsp. almonds, slivered
- 1 garlic clove, mashed
- 1/2 tsp. cumin, ground
- 1/2 tsp. paprika

DIRECTIONS

Step 1

Bring a large saucepan of salted water to a boil over high heat.

Step 2

Cook in it the beans for 32 min. Drain it and transfer it to a saucepan.

Step 3

Add the oil, garlic, cumin, paprika, and cloves. Cook them for 3 min.

Step 4

Stir in the almonds and toss them to coat. Stir in the green beans and adjust their seasoning.

Step 5

Adjust the seasoning of your salad then serve it.

Step 6

Enjoy.

CHICKEN SOUP NORTH AFRICAN

Prep Time: 5 mins

Total Time: 2 hr 5 mins

Servings per Recipe: 6

NUTRITIONAL VALUE

Calories 160.5 , Fat 6.9g , Cholesterol 70.1mg , Sodium 156.4mg , Carbohydrates 12.1g , Protein 12.0g

INGREDIENTS

- 6 chicken drumsticks

- 1 large onion, chopped

- 1 large egg yolk, beaten

- 9 C. water

- 1/4 C. fresh parsley, finely chopped

- 7 oz. canned chickpeas, drained

- 2-3 tsp. olive oil

- 1 cinnamon stick

- 1 1/2 tbsp basmati rice

- 1/2 lemon, juice of

- salt & pepper

DIRECTIONS

Step 1

Place a large pot over medium heat. Heat in it the oil. Cook in it the onion for 3 min.

Step 2

Stir in the chicken with a cinnamon stick. Cook them for 9 min while stirring often.

Step 3

Stir in the water with a pinch of salt and pepper. Put on the lid and cook them for 16 min.

Step 4

Once the time is up, drain the chicken pieces, shred them and discard the bones.

Step 5

Stir them back them back into the pot with chickpeas. Cook them for 10 to 12 min with the lid on.

Step 6

Once the time is up, stir in the water. Adjust the seasoning of your then bring it to a simmer.

Step 7

Get a mixing bowl: Whisk in it the lemon juice with egg yolk.

Step 8

Drizzle it in the pot while stirring. Cook it for 2 min then stir in the parsley.

Step 9

Serve your soup hot.

Step 10

Enjoy.

POTATO SOUP IN ALGERIA

Prep Time: 15 mins

Total Time: 55 mins

Servings per Recipe: 6

NUTRITIONAL VALUE

Calories 31.5 , Fat 2.3g , Cholesterol 3.2mg , Sodium 150.0mg , Carbohydrates 1.0g , Protein 1.6g

INGREDIENTS

- 2 1/4 lb. fish fillet, cubed

- 1 tbsp. cumin

- 2 large potatoes, diced

- 1 tsp. ras el hanout, see appendix

- 2 green bell peppers, diced

- 1 tsp. coriander

- 1 large carrot, diced

- 2 bay leaves

- 1 fennel bulb, diced

- 1 piece lemon rind

- 2 onions, diced

- 1 tbsp. harissa

- 1 celery rib, diced

- 4 tbsp. olive oil

- 4 tbsp. tomato paste

- 8 1/2 C. water or vegetable broth

DIRECTIONS

Step 1

Place a large soup pot over medium heat. Heat in it the oil.

Step 2

Cook in it the onion for 3 min. Stir in the bell peppers, potatoes, carrot, fennel, and celery.

Step 3

Cook them for 3 to 5 min. Stir in the tomato paste and cook them for 30 sec.

Step 4

Stir in the water with bay leaves, seasonings, and lemon rind.

Step 5

Bring them to a simmer then lower the heat and cook them for 22 min.

Step 6

Stir in the fish and cook them for an extra 16 min.

Step 7

Adjust the seasoning of your soup then serve it hot as it is or blend it smooth.

Step 8

Enjoy.

ALGERIAN LAMB SHOULDER

Prep Time: 20 mins

Total Time: 1 hr 40 mins

Servings per Recipe: 4

NUTRITIONAL VALUE

Calories 787.1 , Fat 59.5g , Cholesterol 163.3mg , Sodium 744.0mg , Carbohydrates 22.1g , Protein 42.3g

INGREDIENTS

- 3 tbsp oil

- 2 lbs boneless lamb shoulder, 1-inch chunks

- 1/2 tsp. saffron or 1/2 tsp. turmeric

- 1 medium onion, chopped

- 4 C. water

- 4 garlic cloves, minced

- 1 1/2 lbs green beans, 2-inch pieces

- 1 tsp. salt

- 2 tomatoes, diced

- 1/4 tsp. fresh ground black pepper

- 1 medium onion, sliced in rings

- 1 tsp. ground cumin

- 4 tbsp parsley, chopped

- 1/2 tsp. cayenne pepper

- 1 tsp. ground cumin

DIRECTIONS

Step 1

Place a pot over medium heat. Heat in it the oil.

Step 2

Cook in it the lamb with garlic and onion for 5 min.

Step 3

Stir in the salt, pepper, 1 tsp. cumin, cayenne, and saffron. Cook them for 2 min.

Step 4

Stir in the tomato with water. Heat them until they start boiling. Lower the heat and put on the lid.

Step 5

Cook them for 46 min. Stir in the green beans and cook them for 10 to 12 min.

Step 6

Sir in the onion with parsley and 1 tsp. of cumin. Cook them for an extra 10 to 12 min.

Step 7

Adjust the seasoning of your stew then serve it hot with some couscous.

Step 8

Enjoy.

LAMB TAGINE WITH SAFFRON

Prep Time: 20 mins

Total Time: 3 hr 20 mins

Servings per Recipe: 4

NUTRITIONAL VALUE

Calories 933.8 , Fat 40.6g , Cholesterol 120.0mg , Sodium 923.9mg , Carbohydrates 89.4g , Protein 62.1g

INGREDIENTS

- 2 lbs. lamb, cut into pieces
- 3 tbsps olive oil
- 3 lbs. artichokes
- 1 preserved lemon
- 3 lbs. green peas
- 1/2 lb. olive, green
- 1 tsp ginger
- 1 bunch parsley
- 1 pinch saffron

- lemon juice

- 1 clove garlic

DIRECTIONS

Step 1

Get a large mixing bowl: Mix in it the olive oil with garlic, ginger, and saffron.

Step 2

Add the lamb pieces and toss them to coat.

Step 3

Place a tagine or stew pot over medium heat. Heat in it 1 tbsp of olive oil.

Step 4

Brown in it the meat pieces for 3 to 4 min on each side.

Step 5

Arrange the artichoke hearts on top followed by the olives, preserved lemon, 1/2 C. of water, a pinch of salt and pepper.

Step 6

Put on the lid and let it cook over the lowest heat setting for 1 h 30 min to 2 h until the meat is done.

Step 7

Serve your lamb tagine warm with some bread.

Step 8

Enjoy.

ARABIAN MEATBALL SOUP

Prep Time: 20 mins

Total Time: 2 hr 5 mins

Servings per Recipe: 6

NUTRITIONAL VALUE

Calories 707.9 , Fat 55.9g , Cholesterol 140.6mg , Sodium 1959.0mg , Carbohydrates 18.0g , Protein 33.0g

INGREDIENTS

- Meat

- 2 tbsps olive oil

- Stew

- 1 small yellow onion, minced

- 1/4 C. olive oil

- 1 lb. ground chuck

- 1 lb. beef short rib

- 1 tbsp ground cumin

- kosher salt & ground black pepper

- 1 tbsp ground black pepper

- 4 garlic cloves, chopped

- 1 tbsp cilantro, minced

- 1 large yellow onion, minced

- 1 tbsp parsley, minced

- 5 C. beef stock

- 2 1/4 tsps kosher salt

- 6 oz. spinach leaves, chopped

- 1 1/2 tsps paprika

- 1 (16 oz.) cans white kidney beans, rinsed

- 3/4 tsp ground cinnamon

- drained

- 1 egg, beaten

- cooked couscous

DIRECTIONS

Step 1

To prepare the meatballs:

Step 2

Place a soup pot over high heat. Heat in it 1 tbsp of oil.

Step 3

Cook in it the onion for 6 min. Transfer it to a mixing bowl with the chuck, cumin, pepper, cilantro, parsley, salt, paprika, cinnamon, and egg. Shape the mixture into meatballs.

Step 4

Heat another tbsp of oil in the saucepan. Brown in it the meatballs for 5 min. Drain them and place them aside.

Step 5

To prepare the soup:

Step 6

Sprinkle some salt and pepper all over the ribs. Brown them for 7 min. Drain them and place them aside.

Step 7

Stir the onion with garlic into the saucepan. Let them cook for 6 min.

Step 8

Add the ribs back with stock. Cook them until they start boiling. Lower the heat and let them cook for 60 min.

Step 9

Stir in the meatballs and let them cook for an extra 9 min. Stir in the beans with spinach for 5 min.

Step 10

Adjust the seasoning of your ribs and meatballs stew. Serve it hot.

Step 11

Enjoy.

TUNA GYROS

Prep Time: 10 mins

Total Time: 10 mins

Servings per Recipe: 4

NUTRITIONAL VALUE

Calories 260.3 , Fat 8.8g , Cholesterol 109.4mg , Sodium 644.4mg , Carbohydrates 26.9g , Protein 17.7g

INGREDIENTS

- 1/8 cayenne pepper
- 1/2 C. roasted red pepper, chopped
- 2 tbsps lemon juice
- 2 tbsps drained capers
- 1 tbsp olive oil
- 24 inches pita bread, split open
- 2 hard-boiled eggs, peeled and chopped
- 2 C. packed arugula, chopped
- 1 (6 oz.) cans tuna, drained

- 1 C. halved cherry tomatoes

DIRECTIONS

Step 1

Get a mixing bowl: Toss in it the spices, eggs, tuna, tomato, olive oil, roasted pepper, capers, and arugula.

Step 2

Season them with some salt. Spoon the salad into pita wraps then serve them.

Step 3

Enjoy.

ALGERIAN LEG OF LAMB

Prep Time: 10 mins

Total Time: 2 hr 10 mins

Servings per Recipe: 4

NUTRITIONAL VALUE

Calories 235.8 , Fat 11.9g , Cholesterol 0.0mg , Sodium 828.4mg , Carbohydrates 28.8g , Protein 6.4g

INGREDIENTS

- 4 pieces leg of lamb

- 4 carrots, peeled, chunked

- 1 tsp. curry powder

- 4 yellow zucchini, chunked

- 1 tsp. cumin

- 1 C. chickpeas, soaked overnight

- 1 tsp. ground coriander

- 1 medium onion, diced

- 4 C. water or broth

- 1 tsp. salt

- 3 tbsp. oil

- 1 tsp. ras el hanout, see appendix

DIRECTIONS

Step 1

Place a large soup pot over medium heat. Heat in it the oil.

Step 2

Cook in it the meat with onion for 4 min. Stir in the water with seasonings and chickpeas.

Step 3

Lower the heat and put on the lid. Cook them for 60 min.

Step 4

Once the time is up, stir in the veggies and put on half a cover.

Step 5

Cook them for 60 min until the veggies are done.

Step 6

Adjust the seasoning of you stew then serve it hot.

Step 7

Enjoy.

WHOLE CHICKEN MEDITERRANEAN STYLE

Prep Time: 15 mins

Total Time: 55 mins

Servings per Recipe: 4

NUTRITIONAL VALUE

Calories 356.3 , Fat 23.4g , Cholesterol 100.3mg , Sodium 1393.7mg , Carbohydrates 13.3g , Protein 24.0g

INGREDIENTS

- 1 chicken, cut-up

- 1/4 tsp. thyme

- 2 tsp. salt

- 1 tbsp. parsley, minced

- 1/4 tsp. pepper

- 2 tbsp. butter

- 1/2 C. chicken broth

- 1 garlic clove, crushed

- 1 medium eggplant, pared and diced

- 1 medium onion, chopped

- 2 fresh tomatoes, peeled and chopped

DIRECTIONS

Step 1

Coat the chicken with paprika, 1 tsp. of salt and pepper.

Step 2

Place a large pan over medium heat. Heat in it the butter until it melts.

Step 3

Cook in it the chicken pieces for 3 to 4 min on each side. Drain them and place them aside.

Step 4

Pour the broth into the pan. Stir in the garlic, eggplant, onion, and tomatoes; sprinkle with remaining salt, thyme, and parsley.

Step 5

Heat them until they start boiling. Stir in the chicken and put on the lid.

Step 6

Cook them for 32 min over low heat until it the chicken done. Serve it warm.

Step 7

Enjoy.

MINT AND TOMATO LENTILS WITH LAMB

Prep Time: 15 mins

Total Time: 1 hr 5 mins

Servings per Recipe: 4

NUTRITIONAL VALUE

Calories 368.4 , Fat 1.1g , Cholesterol 0.0mg , Sodium 185.0mg , Carbohydrates 64.4g , Protein 25.9g

INGREDIENTS

- 2 C. green lentils, soaked overnight and
- drained
- 1 tsp. ras el hanout
- 1 onion, finely chopped
- olive oil, to fry
- 3 garlic cloves, minced

- 2 pints water

- 1 carrot, grated

- 1 lamb stock cube or 1 beef stock cube

- 1 courgette, grated

- salt & pepper

- 1 tsp. dried mint

- 4 pieces lamb or 4 pieces chicken

- 1/2 tsp. tomato puree

DIRECTIONS

Step 1

Place a pan over medium heat. Heat in it a splash of oil.

Step 2

Cook in it the garlic with onion for 4 min. Stir in the meat and cook them for another 4 min.

Step 3

Transfer the mixture to a pressure cooker. Stir in the remaining ingredients.

Step 4

Put on the lid and cook them for 40 to 46 min on high pressure.

Step 5

Adjust the seasoning of your stew then serve it hot.

Step 6

Enjoy.

HOW TO MAKE FAVA BEANS

Prep Time: 15 mins

Total Time: 20 mins

Servings per Recipe: 4

NUTRITIONAL VALUE

Calories 144.9 , Fat 5.5g , Cholesterol 7.6mg , Sodium 27.8mg , Carbohydrates 17.9g , Protein 6.8g

INGREDIENTS

- 12 oz. frozen fava beans

- 1 tbsp butter

- 4-5 scallions, sliced

- 1 tbsp chopped cilantro

- 1 tsp chopped of mint

- 1/2-1 tsp ground cumin

- 2 tsps olive oil

- salt

DIRECTIONS

Step 1

Bring a salted pot of water to a boil. Cook it the fava beans for 5 min until they become soft.

Step 2

Strain them and peel them.

Step 3

Place a skillet over medium heat. Heat in it the butter. Cook in it the fava beans with scallions for 3 min.

Step 4

Add the cilantro with mint, cumin, olive oil and a pinch of salt. Cook them for 1 min.

Step 5

Serve your salad right away.

Step 6

Enjoy.

EGG SALAD ALGIERS

Prep Time: 15 mins

Total Time: 15 mins

Servings per Recipe: 8

NUTRITIONAL VALUE

Calories 109.8 , Fat 6.6g , Cholesterol 56.8mg , Sodium 132.5mg , Carbohydrates 4.3g , Protein 8.5g

INGREDIENTS

- 2 tsps red wine vinegar

- 2 tbsps olive oil

- 3 tomatoes, diced

- 3 mint leaves, sliced

- salt and pepper

- 1/2 tsp harissa

- 1 (6 oz.) cans tuna in vegetable oil

- 1 bell pepper, seeded and diced

- 2 hard-boiled eggs, peeled and sliced

- 1/2 small fennel bulb, diced

- 1 tbsp capers

- 1/2 red onion, peeled and diced

- black olives

DIRECTIONS

Step 1

Get a large mixing bowl: Whisk in it the vinegar, olive oil, mint, and harissa.

Step 2

Mix in the pepper, fennel, onion, tomato, a pinch of salt and pepper. Spoon the mixture into a serving plate.

Step 3

Arrange over it the sliced eggs, olives, tuna and capers. Serve your salad immediately.

Step 4

Enjoy.

MY FIRST COUSCOUS

Prep Time: 20 mins

Total Time: 1 hr 50 mins

Servings per Recipe: 3

NUTRITIONAL VALUE

Calories 873.4 , Fat 12.3g , Cholesterol 0.0mg , Sodium 629.2mg , Carbohydrates 165.1g , Protein 28.0g

INGREDIENTS

- 2 C. uncooked couscous

- 1 tbsp chili paste

- 2 tbsps olive oil

- 1/2 tbsp paprika

- 1 large onion, cubed

- 1/2 tbsp cinnamon

- 1 large green pepper, cubed

- 1/2 tbsp cumin

- 1 large zucchini, cubed

- 1 tsp salt and pepper

- 2 potatoes

- 2 carrots

- 14 oz. chickpeas

- 4 tbsps tomato paste

DIRECTIONS

Step 1

Place a large saucepan over medium heat. Heat in it the oil.

Step 2

Cook in it the onion for 3 min. Stir in the tomato paste, chickpeas, and 1 C. of water.

Step 3

Bring them to a rolling boil for 16 min. Stir in the veggies with 4 1/4 C. of water.

Step 4

Cook them until they start boiling. Let them cook for 40 to 46 min over low heat.

Step 5

Get large bowl: Pour over it 1 C. of boiling water with 1 C. of sauce from the stew.

Step 6

Let it sit for 6 min. Strain the couscous from excess liquid. Transfer it to a serving bowl.

Step 7

Spoon the veggies stew over it then serve it warm.

Step 8

Enjoy.

GARLICKY LAMB

Prep Time: 15 mins

Total Time: 50 mins

Servings per Recipe: 4

NUTRITIONAL VALUE

Calories 382.7 , Fat 17.2g , Cholesterol 741.9mg , Sodium 427.9mg , Carbohydrates 13.8g , Protein 42.3g

INGREDIENTS

- 28 oz. fresh lamb liver, 1 inch wide pieces

- 6-8 garlic cloves, minced

- salt & freshly ground black pepper

- 2 C. chopped tinned tomatoes with juice

- 1 C. water

- 1/2 C. chopped fresh coriander

- 2 tbsp. good quality olive oil

- 2-3 tsp. fresh ground cumin

DIRECTIONS

Step 1

Place a large pan over medium heat. Heat in it the oil.

Step 2

Cook in it the liver pieces for 2 to 3 min on each side.

Step 3

Lower the heat and let them cook for an extra 6 min. Stir in the garlic with cumin.

Step 4

Cook them for 1 min while stirring. Stir in the tomato with a pinch of salt and pepper.

Step 5

Cook them for 2 min. Stir in the water and put on the lid. Cook them for 26 min.

Step 6

Once the time is up, add the coriander.

Step 7

Adjust the seasoning of your liver stew then serve it hot with some rice.

Step 8

Enjoy.

FATHIA'S BEAN BOWLS

Prep Time: 15 mins

Total Time: 2 hr 30 mins

Servings per Recipe: 4

NUTRITIONAL VALUE

Calories 832.3 , Fat 43.3g , Cholesterol 187.2mg , Sodium 366.6mg , Carbohydrates 46.6g , Protein 63.3g

INGREDIENTS

- 1 C. dried lima beans, soaked overnight

- chopped

- and drained

- 2 C. chicken stock

- 2 tbsp. olive oil

- 4 C. water

- 26.5 oz. lamb

- 14 oz. chopped tomatoes

- 2 medium brown onions, coarsely

- 4 tbsp. chopped fresh coriander

- chopped

- 2 tbsp. lemon juice

- 2 garlic cloves, crushed

- 2 medium carrots, coarsely chopped

- 2 celery ribs, trimmed and coarsely

DIRECTIONS

Step 1

Place a pot over medium heat. Heat in it the oil.

Step 2

Cook in it the lamb pieces for 2 min on each side.

Step 3

Stir in the veggies and cook them for 4 min. Stir in the stock with water and beans.

Step 4

Heat them until they start boiling. Lower the heat and put on the lid.

Step 5

Cook them for 60 min while discarding the rising foam on top every 30 min.

Step 6

Once the time is up, drain the lamb pieces and shred them.

Step 7

Stir them back into the pot with tomatoes. Put on the lid and cook them for an extra 60 min.

Step 8

Turn off the heat and add the lemon juice with coriander.

Step 9

Adjust the seasoning of your soup then serve it hot.

Step 10

Enjoy.

ALGERIAN CREPES

Prep Time: 10 mins

Total Time: 40 mins

Servings per Recipe: 6

NUTRITIONAL VALUE

Calories 444.7 , Fat 6.8g , Cholesterol 104.3mg , Sodium 225.8mg , Carbohydrates 77.3g , Protein 18.4g

INGREDIENTS

- 2 C. fine semolina
- 1 C. plain flour
- 1 pinch salt

- 1 C. whole wheat flour

- 1 C. warm water

- 3 eggs

- 2 C. milk

- 2 tsp. baking powder

- 1 tbsp. vegetable oil

- 1 tbsp. instant yeast

- 2 tsp. sugar

DIRECTIONS

Step 1

Get a large mixing bowl: Mix in it the semolina with flours, baking powder, yeast, sugar, and salt.

Step 2

Mix in the milk with water. Combine them well until you get a thick batter.

Step 3

Place a skillet over medium heat. Pour in it a ladle of the batter in a circle shape.

Step 4

Let it cook until dries out and have holes all over it without flipping it.

Step 5

Slide it to a serving plate that is covered with a kitchen towel.

Step 6

Repeat the process with the remaining batter.

Step 7

Serve you crepes hot with some butter and honey, jam or chocolate syrup.

Step 8

Enjoy.

ALGERIAN MASH FOR TOAST

Prep Time: 10 mins

Total Time: 30 mins

Servings per Recipe: 6

NUTRITIONAL VALUE

Calories 43.0 , Fat 0.4g , Cholesterol 0.0mg , Sodium 4.3mg , Carbohydrates 10.0g , Protein 1.7g

INGREDIENTS

- 2 eggplants,1/2 inch slices

- 2 garlic cloves, crushed

- 1 tsp. sweet paprika

- 1 1/2 tsp. cumin, ground

- 1/2 tsp. sugar

- 1 tbsp. lemon juice

DIRECTIONS

Step 1

Season the eggplant slices with some salt. Place them in a sieve and let them sit for 32 min.

Step 2

Once the time is up, rinse them and dry them.

Step 3

Place a large skillet over medium heat. Heat in it 1/4 inch of oil.

Step 4

Cook in it the eggplant slices until they become golden brown.

Step 5

Drain them and place them on some paper towels to cool down for few minutes.

Step 6

Finely chop them and place them in a sieve to drain for 5 min.

Step 7

Get a large mixing bowl: Combine in it the chopped eggplant with cumin, sugar, and paprika.

Step 8

Stir them to coat. Pour the mixture into a hot pan and cook them for 2 to 3 min.

Step 9

Stir in the lemon juice with a pinch of salt then serve it hot.

Step 10

Enjoy.

MEDITERRANEAN LAMB STEW

Prep Time: 25 mins

Total Time: 55 mins

Servings per Recipe: 6

NUTRITIONAL VALUE

Calories 547.7 , Fat 31.6g , Cholesterol 191.2mg , Sodium 152.5mg , Carbohydrates 5.5g , Protein 58.1g

INGREDIENTS

- 1/4 C. vegetable oil

- 1 1/2 lbs. cubed lamb stew meat

- 1/2 C. chopped parsley

- 1 1/2 tsp saffron

- 1 tbsp butter

- salt

- 1 lemon, cut into wedges

- pepper

- 1 large onion, chopped

- 1 C. water

DIRECTIONS

Step 1

Place a large pan over medium heat. Heat in the oil. Brown in it the lamb pieces for 4 min on each side.

Step 2

Sprinkle over it the saffron, a pinch of salt and pepper.

Step 3

Stir in the onion with water. Cook them until they start boiling. Lower the heat and put on the lid.

Step 4

Let them cook for 16 min over low heat. Remove the lid and add the butter.

Step 5

Let them cook for 8 min.

Step 6

Garnish your stew the parsley and lemon wedges. Serve it warm.

Step 7

Enjoy.

NORTH AFRICAN FRITTATAS

Prep Time: 15 mins

Total Time: 1 hr 25 mins

Servings per Recipe: 6

NUTRITIONAL VALUE

Calories 230.6 , Fat 15.0g , Cholesterol 268.8mg , Sodium 360.9mg , Carbohydrates 8.8g , Protein 15.5g

INGREDIENTS

- 1 eggplant

- 1/4 tsp ground pepper

- 1 tbsp extra virgin olive oil

- 1/8 tsp ground cinnamon

- 1 medium onion, chopped

- 1 tsp harissa, dissolved in 1 tbsp of water

- 1 medium red bell pepper, diced

- 1/4 lb. gruyere cheese, grated

- 8 large eggs

- 1/2 bunch flat leaf parsley, minced

- 2 garlic cloves, minced

- 1/4 tsp rose water

- 1/2 tsp salt

DIRECTIONS

Step 1

Before you do anything, preheat the oven to 450 F.

Step 2

Use a sharp knife to make slits in the eggplant without cutting it all the way through.

Step 3

Place it on a baking sheet and coat it with olive oil.

Step 4

Roast it in the oven for 22 min. Decrease the oven temperature to 350 min.

Step 5

Place the eggplant aside to lose heat for 10 min. Peel it and dice it.

Step 6

Place a pan over medium heat. Heat in it 1 tbsp of olive oil.

Step 7

Cook in it the bell pepper with onion for 9 min. Stir in the garlic with eggplant, and a pinch of salt.

Step 8

Cook them for an extra 2 min. parsley, rose water, salt, pepper, cinnamon, and harissa.

Step 9

Fold the eggplant mixture into the eggs with cheese. Pour the mixture in a greased baking pan.

Step 10

Cook it in the oven for 32 min. Allow your omelet to rest for 12 min then serve it.

Step 11

Enjoy.

HARISSA AND EGGS SKILLET

Prep Time: 5 mins

Total Time: 40 mins

Servings per Recipe: 4

NUTRITIONAL VALUE

Calories 426.8 , Fat 37.2g , Cholesterol 372.0mg , Sodium 861.3mg , Carbohydrates 10.4g , Protein 14.7g

INGREDIENTS

- 2 sweet green bell peppers, deseeded

- 2 chili peppers, deseeded

- 1 tbsp caraway seed

- 2 fluid oz. tomato paste

- 1 tsp salt

- 24 fluid oz. water

- 1/2 tsp black pepper

- 4 fluid oz. extra virgin olive oil

- 8 large eggs

- 1 tbsp paprika

- 2 tbsp harissa

DIRECTIONS

Step 1

Get a blender: Place in it the chilies with bell pepper. Blend them smooth.

Step 2

Place a skillet over medium heat. Heat in it the oil.

Step 3

Stir in the pepper mixture with tomato paste, harissa, caraway seeds, tomato paste, salt, and pepper.

Step 4

Stir in the water and cook them until they start boiling. Lower the heat and let them cook for 22 min.

Step 5

Spread the sauce in the pan then crack the eggs on top. Put on the lid and let them cook for 16 min over low heat.

Step 6

Serve your eggs skillet warm with some bread.

Step 7

Enjoy.

ALGERIAN CHICKEN THIGHS AND LEGS

Prep Time: 20 mins

Total Time: 1 hr 40 mins

Servings per Recipe: 4

NUTRITIONAL VALUE

Calories 397.5 , Fat 27.6g , Cholesterol 81.7mg , Sodium 2496.8mg , Carbohydrates 16.3g , Protein 23.3g

INGREDIENTS

- 1 tbsp. kosher salt

- 4 medium yellow onions, cut into 12 wedges

- 6 garlic cloves, roughly chopped

- each

- 2 tsp. cumin seeds, crushed

- fresh ground black pepper, to taste

- 2 tsp. paprika

- 1 lemon, thinly sliced crosswise seeds removed 1 tsp. ground turmeric

- 1 1/4 C. green olives, pitted

- 5 tbsp. olive oil

- 1/3 C. fresh cilantro, minced

- 4 skinless chicken thighs

- hot cooked rice

- 4 skinless chicken drumsticks

- 1 tsp. saffron thread, crushed

DIRECTIONS

Step 1

Get a mortar: Mash in it the garlic with salt using a pestle until they become like a paste.

Step 2

Pour them into a mixing bowl and add the cumin, paprika, and turmeric. Add 3 tbsp. of oil and mix them well.

Step 3

Stir in the chicken thighs and drumsticks. Cover them with a cling foil.

Step 4

Let it sit for 4 to 5 min the fridge.

Step 5

Place a large pot over high heat. Heat in it the rest of the oil until it starts shimmering.

Step 6

Fry in it the chicken thighs and drumsticks until they become golden brown.

Step 7

Drain them and place them on paper towels to drain.

Step 8

Stir the onion with saffron, a pinch of salt and pepper into the pot.

Step 9

Cook them for 16 min while stirring. Add the chicken thighs and drumsticks back with lemon slices and 1 C. water.

Step 10

Cook them until they start boiling. Lower the heat and put on the lid.

Step 11

Cook them for 40 to 42 until the chicken is done.

Step 12

Stir in the olives with cilantro. Adjust the seasoning of your stew then serve it hot.

Step 13

Enjoy.

NORTH AFRICAN VEGETABLE SOUP

Prep Time: 20 mins

Total Time: 55 mins

Servings per Recipe: 4

NUTRITIONAL VALUE

Calories 138.6 , Fat 3.9g , Cholesterol 0.0mg , Sodium 434.6mg , Carbohydrates 23.7g , Protein 3.5g

INGREDIENTS

- 1 onion
- 2 garlic cloves
- 1 C. garbanzo beans
- 2 tbsp. cilantro
- 2 tbsp. bulghur wheat
- 2 tbsp. olive oil
- 8 C. water
- 2 carrots, large pieces
- 1 tsp. salt
- 1 large potato, large pieces
- pepper, to taste
- 1 1/2 C. butternut squash, large pieces
- 1 tsp. paprika
- 2 tbsp. tomato paste
- 1 pinch cayenne

DIRECTIONS

Step 1

Place a large skillet over medium heat. Heat in it the oil.

Step 2

Cook in it the garlic with onion for 3 min. Stir in the cilantro with seasonings and veggies.

Step 3

Stir in the water and put on the lid. Cook them for 16 min.

Step 4

Once the time is up, drain the veggies and mash them. Stir them back into the pot.

Step 5

Stir in the tomato paste, garbanzos, and bulghur wheat.

Step 6

Cook them for 12 to 16 min. Adjust the seasoning of your stew then serve it hot.

Step 7

Enjoy.

NAAN ALGERIA

Prep Time: 50 mins

Total Time: 54 mins

Servings per Recipe: 1

NUTRITIONAL VALUE

Calories 183.4 , Fat 9.8g , Cholesterol 0.0mg , Sodium 195.9mg , Carbohydrates 21.8g , Protein 4.0g

INGREDIENTS

- 3 C. finely ground whole wheat flour

- 1 tsp. salt

- 1/2 C. olive oil, divided

- 1 1/2 C. water

- 1 tsp. ground cumin

- 1 tsp. sweet paprika

- 1 tsp. turmeric

DIRECTIONS

Step 1

To prepare the dough:

Step 2

Get a mixing bowl: Combine in it the flour with salt and 2 tbsp. of oil.

Step 3

Add the water gradually while mixing until you get smooth dough.

Step 4

Transfer it t a lightly floured working surface and knead it for 14 min.

Step 5

Grease a large bowl with 2 tbsp. of oil. Shape the dough into a ball and place it in it.

Step 6

Cover it with a cling foil and let it rest for 60 min.

Step 7

Get a mixing bowl: Whisk in it the cumin, paprika, turmeric, and remaining 1/4 C. oil.

Step 8

To prepare the flatbread:

Step 9

Shape the dough into 12 balls. Layover them a cling foil to cover them.

Step 10

Place a dough ball on a lightly floured surface. Roll it into a disk until it becomes thin.

Step 11

Place a griddle over medium heat. Cook in it the bread until it becomes puffy and golden brown on both sides.

Step 12

Repeat the process with the remaining dough.

Step 13

Serve your bread warm or cold with some stew, honey, butter, or olive oil.

Step 14

Enjoy.

POMEGRANATES AND ORANGES

Prep Time: 30 mins

Total Time: 40 mins

Servings per Recipe: 4

NUTRITIONAL VALUE

Calories 263.0 , Fat 0.3g , Cholesterol 0.0mg , Sodium 5.6mg , Carbohydrates 67.0g , Protein 1.4g

INGREDIENTS

- 1 1/2 C. water

- 1 C. sugar

- 1/4 C. thinly sliced peeled ginger

- 4 green cardamom pods

- 3 whole star anise

- 6 any small oranges

- 1/2 C. pomegranate seeds

DIRECTIONS

Step 1

Place a large saucepan over medium heat.

Step 2

Stir in it the water, sugar, ginger, cardamom, and star anise. Cook them until they start boiling.

Step 3

Lower the heat and cook them for 10 to 12 min while stirring often.

Step 4

Turn off the heat and put on the lid. Cook them for 16 min until the mixture becomes syrupy.

Step 5

Strain it and place it in the fridge to lose heat completely for at least 120 min.

Step 6

Peel the oranges and slice them into segments. Transfer them to a serving bowl and add to them the syrup.

Step 7

Let them sit for 60 min with the lid on in the fridge.

Step 8

Garnish them with pomegranate seeds then serve it.

Step 9

Enjoy.

SEMOLINA BREAD WITH CHILI SPREAD

Prep Time: 20 mins

Total Time: 40 mins

Servings per Recipe: 6

NUTRITIONAL VALUE

Calories 799.2 , Fat 26.6g , Cholesterol 0.0mg , Sodium 591.8mg , Carbohydrates 118.2g , Protein 20.7g

INGREDIENTS

- Bread
- 4 vine ripened tomatoes
- 2 lbs. semolina, medium ground
- 1 tbsp. olive oil
- 1 1/2 tsp. salt
- 5 garlic cloves, minced
- 3 C. water
- 1 green chili pepper
- 4 tbsp. olive oil
- salt
- 6 tbsp. olive oil, for frying
- Spread/Dip
- 2 large red bell peppers

DIRECTIONS

Step 1

To prepare the pepper dip/spread:

Step 2

Before you do anything, preheat the oven broiler.

Step 3

Place the bell peppers with tomatoes on a baking sheet.

Step 4

Broil them in the oven for 8 min while flipping them every 2 to 3 min.

Step 5

Allow them to cool down completely then peel them and discard the seeds.

Step 6

Place a large skillet. Heat in it 1 tbsp. of olive oil. Cook in it the garlic with chili for 1 min.

Step 7

Drain them and transfer them to a food processor. Add to them the roasted tomatoes and bell peppers.

Step 8

Pulse them several times until they become finely chopped.

Step 9

Pour the mixture into a bowl and place it in the fridge until ready to serve.

Step 10

To prepare the bread:

Step 11

Get a large mixing bowl: Mix in it the semolina with 4 tbsp. of olive oil and salt.

Step 12

Add the water gradually while mixing until you get smooth elastic dough.

Step 13

Shape it into 6 balls then roll them until they become 1/4 inch thick.

Step 14

Place a large pan over medium heat. Heat in it 1 tbsp. of olive oil.

Step 15

Cook in it the dough circles for 3 to 5 min on each side until they become golden brown.

Step 16

Enjoy.

ALGERIAN FRIES

Prep Time: 20 mins

Total Time: 1 hr 10 mins

Servings per Recipe: 6

NUTRITIONAL VALUE

Calories 332.8 , Fat 13.5g , Cholesterol 53.9mg , Sodium 962.1mg , Carbohydrates 41.6g , Protein 12.2g

INGREDIENTS

- 2 tbsp. oil

- 1/2 C. onion, chopped

- 1/2 tsp. cinnamon

- 1 lb. skinless chicken piece

- 3 C. water

- 10 sprigs flat leaf parsley, leaves only,

- 2 lbs. frozen French fries

- chopped

- 1 egg, beaten

- 1/4 C. chickpeas, cooked

- lemon wedge

- 1 tsp. black pepper

- 1 tsp. salt

DIRECTIONS

Step 1

Place a large skillet over medium heat. Heat in it the 2 tbsp. of oil.

Step 2

Stir in it the onion, chicken, 1/2 the parsley, chickpeas, pepper, salt and cinnamon.

Step 3

Put on the lid and cook them for 10 to 12 min. Stir in the water and cook them until they start boiling.

Step 4

Prepare the French fries by following the instructions on the package.

Step 5

Stir the beaten egg with fries into the pot and cook them for 10 to 12 min.

Step 6

Garnish it with parsley then serve it hot.

Step 7

Enjoy.

LEILA'S DESSERT (PUDDING)

Prep Time: 15 mins

Total Time: 50 mins

Servings per Recipe: 6

NUTRITIONAL VALUE

Calories 519.5 , Fat 23.9g , Cholesterol 0.0mg , Sodium 118.3mg , Carbohydrates 72.5g , Protein 12.1g

INGREDIENTS

- 1/2 lb. dates, pitted and finely chopped

- 1 C. sugar

- 1 C. almonds, blanched & chopped

- 1 C. unsalted dry roasted peanuts

- 4 egg whites, stiffly beaten

DIRECTIONS

Step 1

Before you do anything, preheat the oven to 325 F.

Step 2

Get a mixing bowl: Combine in it the dates, sugar, almonds, and peanuts.

Step 3

Add the egg whites and combine them well. Pour the mixture into a greased baking pan.

Step 4

Bake it for 36 to 42 min. Serve it hot with extra toppings of your choice.

Step 5

Enjoy.

BALSAMIC BEETS

Prep Time: 10 mins

Total Time: 1 hr 10 mins

Servings per Recipe: 4

NUTRITIONAL VALUE

Calories 87.2 , Fat 6.8g , Cholesterol 0.0mg , Sodium 38.6mg , Carbohydrates 6.5g , Protein 0.8g

INGREDIENTS

- 4-6 beetroots
- 1-2 tsp sugar
- 1-2 tbsp balsamic vinegar
- 1/2 lemon, juice
- 2 tbsp olive oil
- salt
- 1 bunch mint leaves, sliced

DIRECTIONS

Step 1

Bring a large saucepan of water to a boil. Cook in it the beetroots until they become soft.

Step 2

Drain them and dice them. sugar, balsamic vinegar, lemon juice, olive oil, and a pinch of salt.

Step 3

Stir in the diced beets with mint. Chill your salad in the fridge until ready to serve.

Step 4

Enjoy.

MARIAM'S SALAD

Prep Time: 10 mins

Total Time: 20 mins

Servings per Recipe: 6

NUTRITIONAL VALUE

Calories 178.3 , Fat 14.9g , Cholesterol 62.1mg , Sodium 140.3mg , Carbohydrates 8.6g , Protein 3.0g

INGREDIENTS

- 1 lb. carrot, peeled and sliced

- 1/4 tsp harissa

- 3 tbsp flat leaf parsley, minced

- 12 black olives

- 1 tsp cumin, ground

- 2 hard-boiled eggs, quartered

- 1/3 C. olive oil

- 1/4 C. red wine vinegar

- 2 garlic cloves

DIRECTIONS

Step 1

Place a large saucepan over medium heat. Bring in it 2 C. of water to a boil.

Step 2

Stir in the carrots with a pinch of salt. Cook them until they become soft then drain them.

Step 3

Get a mixing bowl: Whisk in it the parsley, cumin, olive oil, vinegar, garlic, harissa, salt, and pepper.

Step 4

Add the carrots with eggs, and olives. Toss them to coat.

Step 5

Chill the salad in the fridge for about 30 min then serve it.

Step 6

Enjoy.

SPICY PAN-FRIED BEEF

Prep Time: 10 mins

Total Time: 25 mins

Servings per Recipe: 4

NUTRITIONAL VALUE

Calories 64.8 , Fat 7.0g , Cholesterol 0.0mg , Sodium 12.2mg , Carbohydrates 0.8g , Protein 0.2g

INGREDIENTS

- 4 (6 oz.) filet of beef

- 1 tsp coriander seed, crushed

- 1/2 tsp white peppercorns, crushed

- 1 tsp dried ancho chile powder

- 1 tsp ground cumin

- 2 tbsp olive oil

- salt

DIRECTIONS

Step 1

Place a large pan over medium heat. Heat in it the oil.

Step 2

Get a mixing bowl: Stir in it the coriander, peppercorns, chili powder and cumin.

Step 3

Massage the mixture into the beef fillets. Season them with some salt and pepper.

Step 4

Place them in the hot pan and cook them for 5 to 7 min on each side until they are done. Serve them warm.

Step 5

Enjoy.

MY FIRST TAGINE

Prep Time: 15 mins

Total Time: 2 hr 45 mins

Servings per Recipe: 4

NUTRITIONAL VALUE

Calories 279.1 , Fat 25.2g , Cholesterol 0.0mg , Sodium 83.5mg , Carbohydrates 14.2g , Protein 2.4g

INGREDIENTS

- 7 tbsp. olive oil
- 1 lemon, juice of
- 1/2 C. fresh cilantro, chopped with heavy
- 2 lbs. fish steaks diced
- stems removed
- fresh ground black pepper, to taste

- 4 garlic cloves

- 4 ripe plum tomatoes, halved lengthwise

- 3 inches gingerroot, peeled and chopped

- 1 medium onion, diced

- 2 tsp. ground cumin

- 1 red bell pepper, diced

- 1 tsp. ground coriander

- 1 green bell pepper, diced

- 1/2 tsp. anise seed

- 2 C. eggplants, diced

- 1/4 tsp. cayenne pepper

- 1/4 C. pitted black olives

- salt, to taste

- cilantro leaf, chopped

DIRECTIONS

Step 1

Get a food processor: Combine in it 4 tbsp. of olive oil with cilantro, garlic, ginger, cumin, coriander, anise, cayenne pepper, 1/4 tsp. salt and lemon juice.

Step 2

Blend them smooth. Pour the mixture into a large mixing bowl.

Step 3

Add the fish cubes and toss them to coat. Put on the lid and let them sit in the fridge for 120 min.

Step 4

Before you do anything else, preheat the oven to 300 F.

Step 5

Arrange the tomatoes in a roasting dish. Drizzle over them 1 tbsp. of olive oil with a pinch of salt.

Step 6

Place it in the oven and let it cook for 1 h 30 min.

Step 7

Drain the tomatoes and roughly chop them.

Step 8

Place a large pan over medium heat. Heat in it the rest of the oil.

Step 9

Cook in it the peppers with onion. Cook them for 6 min. Stir in the eggplant and cook them for 6 min.

Step 10

Stir in the olives with tomatoes, a pinch of salt and pepper.

Step 11

Transfer the mixture to a baking pan. Top it with the fish cubes.

Step 12

Put on the lid and bake it for 22 to 32 min. Serve it hot.

Step 13

Enjoy.

NORTH AFRICAN HANDMADE SAUSAGE

Prep Time: 35 mins

Total Time: 35 mins

Servings per Recipe: 1

NUTRITIONAL VALUE

Calories 306.9 , Fat 22.5g , Cholesterol 78.1mg , Sodium 306.6mg , Carbohydrates 5.8g , Protein 19.9g

INGREDIENTS

- 2 lbs. boneless lamb, ground

- 4 oz. lamb, fat attached to the lamb kidney

- 1 tbsp. red hot chili powder

- 2 heads garlic, peeled and minced

- 2 tbsp. sweet paprika

- 1 tsp. salt

- 1 C. cold water

- 1 tsp. black pepper

- 1 small lamb intestine casing

- 1 tbsp. ground cumin

- 1 tbsp. ground coriander

- 1 tbsp. sumac

DIRECTIONS

Step 1

Get a food processor: Combine in it the fat from the lamb kidney with garlic and ground lamb.

Step 2

Pulse them several times until they become smooth.

Step 3

Add the cumin, coriander, sumac, chili powder, paprika, salt, pepper, and water.

Step 4

Processor them until they become smooth.

Step 5

Spoon the mixture into the casing while twisting it after measuring 4 inches.

Step 6

Fry them in a pan, or grill them then serve them hot.

Step 7

Enjoy.

PEPPER AND TOMATO BOREK

Prep Time: 40 mins

Total Time: 1 hr

Servings per Recipe: 10

NUTRITIONAL VALUE

Calories 342.0 , Fat 3.6g , Cholesterol 0.0mg , Sodium 4.0mg , Carbohydrates 66.1g , Protein 10.2g

INGREDIENTS

- Filling

- Pastry

- 4 onions, sliced

- 17.5 oz. fine semolina

- 2 tbsp. concentrated tomato puree

- 9 oz. plain flour

- 2 green peppers, strips

- salt

- 2 tbsp. olive oil

- water

- salt & pepper

- 1 hot pepper

DIRECTIONS

Step 1

To prepare the filling:

Step 2

Place a large skillet over medium heat. Heat in it the oil.

Step 3

Cook in it the peppers with onion for 3 min. Stir in the tomato puree with a pinch of salt and pepper.

Step 4

Cook them for 6 min. turn off the heat and let the mixture cool down completely.

Step 5

To prepare the pastry:

Step 6

Combine in it the flour with semolina. Add a pinch of salt and a drizzle of olive oil. Mix them well.

Step 7

Add water gradually while mixing until you get stiff dough. Knead it for 10 min while adding more water until it becomes soft and elastic.

Step 8

Shape it into balls in the shape of a golf ball. Place one of them on an oiled working surface until it becomes thin.

Step 9

Put in the middle of it 2 tsp. of the filling. Pull the dough sides over the filling in the shape of a square.

Step 10

Place a large skillet over medium heat. Heat in it a splash of vegetable oil.

Step 11

Cook in it the pastry until it becomes golden brown on both sides.

Step 12

Repeat the process with the remaining dough and filling. Serve them warm.

Step 13

Enjoy.

ALGERIANNPOACHED EGGS (SHAKSHOUKA II)

Prep Time: 1 hr 35 mins

Total Time: 3 hr 35 mins

Servings per Recipe: 8

NUTRITIONAL VALUE

Calories 908.7 , Fat 29.0g , Cholesterol 70.3mg , Sodium 473.1mg , Carbohydrates 125.0g , Protein 34.9g

INGREDIENTS

- 1 yellow onion, chopped

- 8 lamb chops or 8 skinless chicken pieces

- 1 C. chickpeas, drained

- 3 garlic cloves, chopped

- 2 tsp. ras el hanout spice mix

- 2 medium carrots, sliced

- salt & pepper

- 2 medium zucchini, sliced

- 1 pinch dried mint

- 2 large potatoes, diced

- 1 tbsp. sunflower oil or 1 tbsp. vegetable oil 1/4 swede or 1/4 turnip, diced

- 1 C. of liquidized tomato puree

- 1 parsnip, diced

- 6 1/2 C. water

- 1 large green chili, roughly chopped

DIRECTIONS

Step 1

Place a large skillet over medium heat. Heat in it the oil.

Step 2

Stir in it ras el hanout with meat. Cook them for 3 min.

Step 3

Stir in the zucchini, with parsnip, carrot, potato, and swede.

Step 4

Stir in 4 C. of water with chili pepper, a pinch of salt and pepper.

Step 5

Put on the lid and lower the heat. Cook it for 42 min.

Step 6

Stir in the chickpeas with dry mint, and 2 1/2 C. water. Cook it for an extra 32 min with the lid on.

Step 7

Adjust the seasoning of your soup then serve it hot.

Step 8

Enjoy.

NORTH AFRICAN ORANGE GRILLED CHICKEN

Prep Time: 25 mins

Total Time: 25 mins

Servings per Recipe: 4

NUTRITIONAL VALUE

Calories 556.3 , Fat 38.2g , Cholesterol 150.9mg , Sodium 143.2mg , Carbohydrates 15.3g , Protein 37.1g

INGREDIENTS

- 4 tbsp harissa

- 2 tbsp olive oil

- 16-20 chicken wings

- 4 blood oranges, quartered

- salt

- icing sugar

- cilantro, chopped

DIRECTIONS

Step 1

Before you do anything, preheat the grill and grease it.

Step 2

Get a mixing bowl: Whisk in it the oil with harissa.

Step 3

Season the chicken wings with some salt and pepper. Coat them with the oil mixture.

Step 4

Place them on the grill and let them cook for 6 to 9 min on each side.

Step 5

Coat the blood orange wedges with icing sugar. Grill them until they become charred.

Step 6

Serve your chicken wings next to the grilled orange wedges.

Step 7

Enjoy.

GARBANZO SOUP BOWLS

Prep Time: 8 hr

Total Time: 11 hr

Servings per Recipe: 8

NUTRITIONAL VALUE

. Calories 168.7 , Fat 8.2g , Cholesterol 23.2mg , Sodium 100.1mg , Carbohydrates 18.2g , Protein 6.5g

INGREDIENTS

- 230 g dried garbanzo beans, soaked

- overnight

- person

- 2 C. vegetarian beef broth

- harissa, with some water

- 4 garlic cloves

- 1 pinch ground cumin

- 3 tbsp extra virgin olive oil

- ground pepper

- salt

- 16 olives

- pepper

- capers

- 8 eggs, hard-boiled and peeled

- diced roasted red pepper

- 1/2 C. day-old French bread, cubed per

- extra virgin olive oil

- 1 lemon wedge, per person

DIRECTIONS

Step 1

Before you do anything, preheat the oven to 200 F.

Step 2

Place an ovenproof pot over high heat. Stir in it the chickpeas with garlic, oil, stock salt, and pepper.

Step 3

Cover them with water. Cook them until they start boiling. Put on the lid and transfer the pot to the oven.

Step 4

Let them cook for 3 h.

Step 5

Place a slice of bread in each serving bowl. Pour over it the chickpea soup followed by the hard-boiled egg.

Step 6

Drizzle some harissa on top with olives, cumin, and extra toppings of your choice.

Step 7

Serve your soup bowl warm with some lemon wedges on the side.

Step 8

Enjoy.

CAYENNE CARROT APPETIZER

Prep Time: 15 mins

Total Time: 30 mins

Servings per Recipe: 4

NUTRITIONAL VALUE

Calories 166.9 , Fat 10.8g , Cholesterol 0.0mg , Sodium 121.7mg , Carbohydrates 17.0g , Protein 1.8g

INGREDIENTS

- 1 1/2 lbs. carrots, peeled, cut into rounds
- 1/2 C. water

- 3 tbsp olive oil

- 3 tbsp white vinegar

- 2 1/4 tsp ground cumin

- 1/3 C. chopped cilantro

- 1/4 tsp cayenne pepper

DIRECTIONS

Step 1

Bring a salted saucepan of water to a boil. Cook in it the carrots until they become soft. Drain them.

Step 2

Place a large pan over medium heat. Heat in it the oil. Cook in it the cayenne pepper with cumin for 20 sec.

Step 3

Stir in the carrots with water and vinegar. Cook them for 4 min.

Step 4

Adjust the seasoning of your salad then stir in the cilantro. Serve it warm.

Step 5

Enjoy.

ALGERIAN GLAZED ROUNDED FLATBREAD

Prep Time: 20 mins

Total Time: 1 hr 15 mins

Servings per Recipe: 15

NUTRITIONAL VALUE

Calories 348.8 , Fat 18.8g , Cholesterol 101.0mg , Sodium 194.5mg , Carbohydrates 43.2g , Protein 4.3g

INGREDIENTS

- Flatbread

- 1 C. egg

- Syrup

- 1 C. sugar

- 2 C. granulated sugar

- 1 C. butter or 1 C. margarine

- 4 C. water

- 1 C. of freshly ground almonds

- 1 1/2 tbsp. orange blossom water

- 1 C. stale bread

- 1 1/2 tsp. baking powder

- 1 lemon, zest of, large

- 1/2 tsp. vanilla essence

DIRECTIONS

Step 1

Before you do anything, preheat the oven to 350 F

Step 2

To prepare the syrup:

Step 3

Place a heavy saucepan over medium heat. Combine in it the water with sugar.

Step 4

Heat in it until it starts boiling. Stir in the blossom water and cook them for 2 min.

Step 5

Turn off the heat and let the syrup cool down completely.

Step 6

To prepare the bread:

Step 7

Get a large mixing bowl: Cream in it the eggs in until they become pale.

Step 8

Add the sugar with butter and beat them until they become smooth **Step 9**

Stir in the bread with almonds, lemon zest, and vanilla extract.

Step 10

Pour the batter into a greased baking pan. Bake it for 42 min until it becomes golden.

Step 11

Once the time is up, pour the syrup over the hot bread. Let it sit in the turned off oven for 6 min.

Step 12

Once the time is up, serve it warm with toppings of your choice.

Step 13

Enjoy.

HOT CHICKPEA SALAD

Prep Time: 15 mins

Total Time: 35 mins

Servings per Recipe: 6

NUTRITIONAL VALUE

Calories 226.2 , Fat 6.1g , Cholesterol 0.0mg , Sodium 543.2mg , Carbohydrates 39.9g , Protein 6.2g

INGREDIENTS

- 1 1/2 lbs. carrots, quartered and sliced
- 1/2 tsp ground cumin
- 2 tbsp golden raisins
- 1/2 tsp salt
- 2 tbsp canola oil
- 19 oz. chickpeas, drained and rinsed
- 2 onions, sliced
- 1 pinch cayenne pepper
- 1/2 tsp hot red pepper flakes
- 1 lemon
- 1/2 tsp caraway seed
- 1/2 tsp paprika

DIRECTIONS

Step 1

Place a large salted saucepan of water to a boil. Cook in it the carrots until they become soft.

Step 2

Drain them and place them aside to cool down for a while. Place 1/2 C. of the cooking water aside.

Step 3

Get a mixing bowl: Place in it the raisins and cover them with hot water. Let them sit for 12 min then drain them.

Step 4

Place a skillet over medium heat. Heat in it the oil. Cook in it the onion for 12 min.

Step 5

Stir in the raisins with carrot water, red pepper flakes, caraway seeds, cumin, paprika, and a pinch of salt.

Step 6

Cook them until they start boiling. Stir in the carrot slices and let them cook for 5 min.

Step 7

Add the chickpeas with a pinch of cayenne pepper. Cook them for 3 min.

Step 8

Serve your chickpeas salad warm with some lemon wedges.

Step 9

Enjoy.

POTATO SALAD IN NORTH AFRICA

Prep Time: 15 mins

Total Time: 30 mins

Servings per Recipe: 4

NUTRITIONAL VALUE

Calories 208.2 , Fat 7.5g , Cholesterol 1.9mg , Sodium 18.9mg , Carbohydrates 32.6g , Protein 4.3g

INGREDIENTS

- 1 1/2 lbs. potatoes
- 1/4 tsp harissa, see appendix
- 1 tsp ground cumin

- 1 large lemon, juice

- 2 tbsp extra virgin olive oil

- 1/4 C. plain yogurt

- 2 tbsp cilantro, minced

DIRECTIONS

Step 1

Bring a large salted saucepan of water to a boil. Cook in it the potatoes until they become soft.

Step 2

Drain them, peel them and dice them.

Step 3

Get a mixing bowl: Mix in it the harissa with lemon juice, cumin, oil, yogurt, and cilantro.

Step 4

Add the potatoes with a pinch of salt and pepper. Toss them to coat.

Step 5

Serve your salad chilled or warm.

Step 6

Enjoy.

GINGER SHRIMP

Prep Time: 15 mins

Total Time: 20 mins

Servings per Recipe: 4

NUTRITIONAL VALUE

Calories 240.0 , Fat 14.9g , Cholesterol 220.8mg , Sodium 258.8mg , Carbohydrates 1.5g , Protein 24.1g

INGREDIENTS

- 1 lb. unshelled shrimp, peeled

- 1 bunch cilantro, chopped

- 2 garlic cloves, chopped

- salt and pepper

- 4 tbsp olive oil

- lemon wedge

- 1 tsp cumin

- 1/2 tsp ground ginger

- 1 tsp paprika

- 1/4 tsp cayenne

DIRECTIONS

Step 1

Before you do anything, preheat the oven broiler.

Step 2

Use a knife to cut a slit in the middle of the shrimp in the shape of a butterfly.

Step 3

Get a mixing bowl: Whisk in it the oil with garlic, cumin, ginger, paprika, cayenne, cilantro, a pinch of salt and pepper.

Step 4

Place the shrimp on a baking tray. Drizzle over them the oil mixture and toss them to coat.

Step 5

Cook the shrimp in the oven broiler for 5 min. Serve them warm with some lemon.

Step 6

Enjoy.

*

* 64

NORTH AFRICAN FLORETS

Prep Time: 5 mins

Total Time: 25 mins

Servings per Recipe: 4

NUTRITIONAL VALUE

Calories 171.1 , Fat 13.8g , Cholesterol 0.0mg , Sodium 628.3mg , Carbohydrates 11.0g , Protein 3.6g

INGREDIENTS

* 8 oz. tomatoes, chopped

* 2 large garlic cloves, finely chopped

* 4 tbsp. olive oil

* 1 tsp. paprika

* 1 tsp. salt

* 1 tsp. black pepper

* 1 tsp. harissa

* 1 cauliflower, medium-sized, trimmed, cut

* into florets

DIRECTIONS

Step 1

Bring a large salted pot of water to a boil. Cook in it the cauliflower for 8 min.

Step 2

Place a small pan over medium heat. Heat in it the oil. Cook in it the garlic 1 min.

Step 3

Stir in the tomatoes, salt, pepper, paprika, and harissa. Lower the heat and cook them for 10 to 12 min.

Step 4

Once the time is up, drain the cauliflower and add it to the pan.

Step 5

Toss them to coat and serve them hot.

Step 6

Enjoy.

LAMB BATNA

Prep Time: 10 mins

Total Time: 1 hr 10 mins

Servings per Recipe: 8

NUTRITIONAL VALUE

Calories 350.0 , Fat 19.6g , Cholesterol 86.4mg , Sodium 96.6mg , Carbohydrates 23.4g , Protein

- 21.0g

INGREDIENTS

- 2 1/2 lbs. lamb, cubed

- 3 tbsp. butter

- 2 tbsp. raisins

- 1/2 tsp. ground cinnamon

- 2 tbsp. almonds

- 3 C. water

- 1 pear, peeled and cubed

- 1/4 C. sugar

- 1/4 C. orange juice

- 16 prunes, soaked and drained

- 1 tsp. orange blossom water

DIRECTIONS

Step 1

Place a large skillet over medium heat. Heat in it the butter until it melts.

Step 2

Cook in it the lamb for 6 min. Stir in the cinnamon with sugar and water.

Step 3

Cook them for 42 min while stirring often with the lid on.

Step 4

Once the time is up, stir in the prunes, raisins, almonds, pear, and orange blossom water.

Step 5

Cook them for an extra 16 min until the sauce becomes thick.

Step 6

Stir in the orange juice and cook it for 5 min.

Step 7

Adjust the seasoning of your stew then serve it hot.

Step 8

Enjoy.

HOT CARROT MASH

Prep Time: 20 mins

Total Time: 35 mins

Servings per Recipe: 4

NUTRITIONAL VALUE

Calories 205.8 , Fat 14.2g , Cholesterol 0.0mg , Sodium 720.5mg , Carbohydrates 19.7g , Protein 2.0g

INGREDIENTS

- 1 3/4 lbs. carrots, peeled and chopped

- 1 tsp salt

- 1/4 C. olive oil

- 3 tbsp white wine vinegar

- 1 garlic clove, crushed

- 1 tsp harissa

- 2 tsp cumin, ground

- black olives

DIRECTIONS

Step 1

Place a large salted saucepan of water over medium heat. Bring it to a boil.

Step 2

Cook in it the carrots until they become soft. Drain them and mash them with a food processor or potato masher.

Step 3

Get a mixing bowl: Combine in it the mashed carrots with olive oil, vinegar, garlic, seasoning, and harissa.

Step 4

Adjust the seasoning of your carrot mash then serve it with some toast.

Step 5

Enjoy.

RADISH SALAD

Prep Time: 15 mins

Total Time: 15 mins

Servings per Recipe: 2

NUTRITIONAL VALUE

Calories 486.1 , Fat 34.6g , Cholesterol 201.3mg , Sodium 839.0mg , Carbohydrates 10.7g , Protein 32.9g

INGREDIENTS

- 2 eggs, hard-boiled, peeled and chopped
- 3 tbsp olive oil
- 1 tomato, chopped
- 1 tbsp white vinegar
- 1 green pepper, chopped
- 1 tbsp dried mint
- 1/2 yellow onion, chopped

- 1/4 tsp salt

- 1-2 jalapeno, chopped

- 1 (6 oz.) cans tuna packed in oil, drained

- 5 radishes, chopped

- feta cheese

- 10 olives, chopped

DIRECTIONS

Step 1

Get a mixing bowl: Whisk in it the olive oil with vinegar, mint, and salt.

Step 2

Add the remaining ingredients and toss them to coat.

Step 3

Adjust the seasoning of your salad then serve it.

Step 4

Enjoy.

ALGIERS CAFE COUSCOUS

Prep Time: 15 mins

Total Time: 1 hr 35 mins

Servings per Recipe: 4

NUTRITIONAL VALUE

Calories 361.6 , Fat 2.5g , Cholesterol 0.0mg , Sodium 681.7mg , Carbohydrates 75.6g , Protein 13.3g

INGREDIENTS

- 1 large onion, chopped

- 1/2 tsp. turmeric

- 3-4 whole cloves

- 1/4 tsp. cayenne

- 3 medium zucchini

- 1/2 C. vegetable stock

- 4 small yellow squash

- 1/2 tbsp. cinnamon

- 3/4 large carrot

- 1 1/2 tsp. black pepper

- 4 medium yellow potatoes, skins on

- 1/2 tsp. salt

- 1 red bell pepper

- 5 tbsp. tomato puree

- 1 (15 oz.) cans garbanzo beans

- 1 C. couscous

DIRECTIONS

Step 1

Place a pot over medium heat. Stir in it a splash of stock with onion.

Step 2

Cook it for 3 min. Stir in the seasonings and cook them for 2 min while stirring.

Step 3

Stir in the tomato paste and cook them for 2 min.

Step 4

Stir in the veggies with a pinch of cinnamon. Cover them with water and heat them until they start boiling.

Step 5

Lower the heat and put on the lid. Cook them for 60 min over low heat.

Step 6

Once the time is up, stir in the garbanzo beans and cook them for 5 to 6 min.

Step 7

To make the couscous add it to a bowl with just enough boiling water to cover everything. Let the mix sit for about 10 mins.

Step 8

Fluff it with a fork and transfer it to a serving plate.

Step 9

Pour over it the veggies stew then serve it hot.

Step 10

Enjoy.

COUSCOUS GHARDAÏA

Prep Time: 15 mins

Total Time: 30 mins

Servings per Recipe: 6

NUTRITIONAL VALUE

Calories 226.4 , Fat 5.6g , Cholesterol 1.5mg , Sodium 86.0mg , Carbohydrates 38.6g , Protein 6.9g

INGREDIENTS

- 2 tbsp. olive oil

- 1 medium onion, chopped

- 1/2 tsp. ground coriander

- 8 oz. mushrooms, sliced

- 1 lemon, zest of

- 1 grated carrot

- 1 lemon, juice of

- 2 garlic cloves, minced

- 1/2 C. raisins

- 1/2 tsp. cumin

- 1 1/4 C. chicken stock

- 1 C. couscous

DIRECTIONS

Step 1

Place a large skillet over medium heat. Heat in it the oil.

Step 2

Cook in it the onion with carrots and mushrooms for 5 min.

Step 3

Stir in the seasonings with lemon zest, raisins, and couscous. Cook them for 2 min.

Step 4

Stir in the lemon juice with stock. Lower the heat and cook them for 3 to 4 min.

Step 5

Put on the lid and turn off the heat. Let it sit for 5 to 6 min. Serve it warm.

Step 6

Enjoy.

ALGERIAN LUNCH BOX (MINT SALAD)

Prep Time: 15 mins

Total Time: 15 mins

Servings per Recipe: 2

NUTRITIONAL VALUE

Calories 301.6 , Fat 30.7g , Cholesterol 0.0mg , Sodium 353.5mg , Carbohydrates 8.0g , Protein 1.5g

INGREDIENTS

- 1 large cucumber, peeled, halved lengthwise, seeded, thinly sliced

- 3 1/2 tsp. white wine vinegar

- 1/2 green capsicum, cored, seeded and cut

- salt & freshly ground black pepper

- in half lengthwise

- 1/3 C. pitted and coarsely chopped green

- olives

- 4 large fresh mint leaves, finely chopped

- 2 tbsp. finely chopped fresh coriander

- leaves (cilantro)

- 1/2 tsp. paprika

- 1/4 C. extra virgin olive oil

DIRECTIONS

Step 1

Get a mixing bowl: Combine in it the cucumber with green pepper, olives, and mint.

Step 2

Stir in the coriander, paprika, olive oil, and vinegar.

Step 3

Sprinkle over them some salt and pepper then stir them well.

Step 4

Serve your salad right away.

Step 5

Enjoy.

TOMATO BRAISED EGG SKILLET (SHAKSHOUKA I)

Prep Time: 10 mins

Total Time: 30 mins

Servings per Recipe: 4

NUTRITIONAL VALUE

Calories 252.8 , Fat 15.5g , Cholesterol 186.0mg , Sodium 85.8mg , Carbohydrates 20.5g , Protein 9.4g

INGREDIENTS

- 3 tbsp. olive oil

- add more red and green bell pepper

- 1/2 tsp. cumin seed

- 1-2 chili pepper, for those that like heat

- 1 tbsp. paprika

- 1 C. water

- 1 onion, thinly sliced

- kosher salt

- 1 tbsp. harissa, for a spicier, deeper flavor fresh ground pepper

- 2-3 garlic cloves, minced

- 4 eggs

- 3 tomatoes, peeled, seeded and diced

- parsley or cilantro, chopped

- 1 potato, small diced cubes

- black olives

- 1 green bell pepper, diced

- capers

- 1 red bell pepper, diced

- 1 yellow bell pepper, diced, if not using

DIRECTIONS

Step 1

Place a large pan over medium heat. Heat in it the oil.

Step 2

Cook in it the cumin seeds for 20 sec. Add the paprika and cook them for 10 sec.

Step 3

Stir in the garlic with the onion and cook them for 6 min.

Step 4

Stir in the tomato and cook them until they start simmering. Stir in the peppers with potato, water, salt, and pepper.

Step 5

Lower the heat and put on the lid. Cook them for 12 min while adding more water if needed.

Step 6

Once the time is up, crack the eggs on top and put on the lid. Cook them for 10 to 12 min until they are done.

Step 7

Serve your chakchouka pan hot with some bread.

Step 8

Enjoy.

MYRIAM'S SALAD

Prep Time: 10 mins

Total Time: 50 mins

Servings per Recipe: 2

NUTRITIONAL VALUE

Calories 93.4 , Fat 2.9g , Cholesterol 0.0mg , Sodium 14.1mg , Carbohydrates 16.7g , Protein 3.2g

INGREDIENTS

- 3 large green bell peppers

- 2 vine ripened tomatoes

- 1-2 garlic clove, minced

- 2-3 tbsp. water

- 1 tsp. olive oil

- salt

- vinegar

DIRECTIONS

Step 1

Place the bell peppers on the stove and grill them until they become black.

Step 2

Transfer them to a plastic bag and seal it. Let it rest for 5 to 6 min.

Step 3

Once the time is up, peel them, rinse them and chop them.

Step 4

Place a skillet over medium heat. Heat in it the oil.

Step 5

Stir in it the tomatoes with peppers and garlic. Cook them for 3 min.

Step 6

Stir in a pinch of salt and cook them for 16 min while often stirring.

Step 7

Serve your tomato salad warm.

Step 8

Enjoy.

ALGERIAN BREAD

Prep Time: 2 hr

Total Time: 2 hr 35 mins

Servings per Recipe: 1

NUTRITIONAL VALUE

Calories 18656.0 , Fat 1800.5g , Cholesterol 554.9mg , Sodium 4767.1mg , Carbohydrates 562.0g , Protein 107.9g

INGREDIENTS

- 3 1/2 C. fine semolina
- 2 tsp. salt
- 1 1/4 C. strong white bread flour
- 2 large egg yolks, beaten
- 2 C. water, room temp. plus extra
- 2-3 tbsp. sesame seeds
- 4 fluid oz. sunflower oil (or vegetable,
- 1 tbsp. nigella seeds
- canola etc.)
- 7 g fast action yeast
- 1 large egg, beaten
- 2 tsp. sugar

DIRECTIONS

Step 1

Get a large mixing bowl: Combine in it the semolina, flour, yeast, sugar, and salt.

Step 2

Add the beaten eggs in the middle with oil and 1 C. of water.

Step 3

Combine them well and knead them until you get a soft dough while adding more water if needed it for about 30 min.

Step 4

Transfer the dough to a greased baking pan and press into an even level.

Step 5

Top it with some extra semolina then lay over it wet towel and let it rest until it doubles in size.

Step 6

Before you do anything, preheat the oven to 356 F.

Step 7

Coat the top of the dough with egg yolks and sesame seeds. Bake it for 35 to 36 min until it becomes golden.

Step 8

Allow your semolina bread to lose heat for at least 8 min. Serve it warm.

Step 9

Enjoy.

HOT BROAD BEANS

Prep Time: 5 mins

Total Time: 50 mins

Servings per Recipe: 4

NUTRITIONAL VALUE

Calories 277.7 , Fat 10.8g , Cholesterol 0.0mg , Sodium 1140.1mg , Carbohydrates 33.1g , Protein 14.2g

INGREDIENTS

- 2 1/4 lb broad bean in the pod, trimmed

- and bite-size pieces

- 1/8 tsp. black pepper

- 1 bunch fresh cilantro, chopped

- salt (1/2 tsp. minimum)

- 6 garlic cloves, peeled and minced

- 1-1 1/2 tsp. vinegar

- 3-4 tbsp olive oil

- 600 ml water

- 1 tsp. paprika

- 1/4 tsp. cayenne

DIRECTIONS

Step 1

Place a large pot over medium heat. Heat in it the oil.

Step 2

Cook in it the garlic with beans for 3 min. Stir in the remaining ingredients and put on the lid.

Step 3

Cook them for 26 to 32 min until the sauce becomes thick. Serve it hot.

Step 4

Enjoy.

PICNIC RICE WITH VINAIGRETTE

Prep Time: 10 mins

Total Time: 2 hr 10 mins

Servings per Recipe: 6

NUTRITIONAL VALUE

Calories 486.9 , Fat 27.5g , Cholesterol 0.0mg , Sodium 13.5mg , Carbohydrates 54.3g , Protein 4.8g

INGREDIENTS

- Vinaigrette

- 1/4 C. vinegar

- 1 (2 oz) jars pimientos, chopped

- 3/4 C. salad oil

- 1/2 onion, chopped

- 1 tsp. Dijon mustard

- 2 C. rice, cook and chilled

- 1 tsp. chopped parsley

- salt and pepper

- 1 tsp. chopped chives

- Garnish

- Salad

- hard-boiled egg

- 1 1/2 green peppers, chopped

- mushroom

- olive

DIRECTIONS

Step 1

To prepare the vinaigrette:

Step 2

Get a mixing bowl: Mix in it all the ingredients.

Step 3

Mix in it the onion with pimento, rice, a pinch of salt and pepper.

Step 4

Toss them to coat and transfer them to a greased baking dish.

Step 5

Press it down then place it in the fridge until ready to serve.

Step 6

Slice it into bars then serve it.

Step 7

Enjoy.

NORTH AFRICAN STYLE CARROTS

Prep Time: 10 mins

Total Time: 40 mins

Servings per Recipe: 4

NUTRITIONAL VALUE

Calories 148.2 , Fat 10.6g , Cholesterol 0.0mg , Sodium 87.1mg , Carbohydrates 13.1g , Protein 1.4g

INGREDIENTS

- 17.5 oz. Carrots, peeled and sliced

- 3 tbsp. oil

- 3 garlic cloves, minced

- 1 hot pepper

- 1/2 tsp. caraway seed

- 1 tsp. paprika

- 1 1/2 tbsp. vinegar

- salt and black pepper

DIRECTIONS

Step 1

Bring a large salted saucepan of water to a boil. Cook in it the carrots for 10 to 14 until they become soft.

Step 2

Combine the garlic with hot pepper, red pepper, caraway seeds and salt. Grind them until they become like a paste.

Step 3

Transfer the mixture to a mixing bowl. Stir into it 1 tbsp. of water with oil. Mix them well.

Step 4

Drain the carrots and transfer them to a skillet. Pour over them the pepper sauce and put on the lid.

Step 5

Cook them for 3 to 4 min then serve them warm.

Step 6

Enjoy.

TOMATO BASED CHICKEN AND CHICKPEAS

Prep Time: 5 mins

Total Time: 55 mins

Servings per Recipe: 4

NUTRITIONAL VALUE

Calories 219.0 , Fat 4.0g , Cholesterol 7.2mg , Sodium 664.6mg , Carbohydrates 34.2g , Protein 11.5g

INGREDIENTS

- 8 chicken pieces

- 2 allspice berries

- 1 small onion, Chopped

- 2 tsp. tomato paste

- 4 garlic cloves, crushed

- 400 g chickpeas, drained

- 1/2 tsp. ras el hanout spice mix

- 2 pints chicken stock

- 1/4 tsp. harissa

DIRECTIONS

Step 1

Place a large saucepan over medium heat. Heat in it 2 tbsp. of oil.

Step 2

Brown in it the chicken pieces for 4 to 5 min on each side.

Step 3

Stir in the garlic, spices, salt, tomato puree and Harissa. Let them cook for 2 to 3 min.

Step 4

Stir in the stock and heat them until they start boiling.

Step 5

Lower the heat and let them cook for 32 min.

Step 6

Stir in the chickpeas and cook them for 10 to 12 min until the stew becomes thick.

Step 7

Adjust the seasoning of your stew then serve it.

Step 8

Enjoy.

PEPPER AND EGG SALAD

Prep Time: 20 mins

Total Time: 20 mins

Servings per Recipe: 4

NUTRITIONAL VALUE

Calories 218.4 , Fat 15.6g , Cholesterol 98.3mg , Sodium 385.1mg , Carbohydrates 13.6g , Protein 7.2g

INGREDIENTS

- 2 sweet red peppers, chopped fine

- 4 medium ripe tomatoes, chopped

- 1 tsp. chopped fresh basil

- 3/4 C. sliced cucumber

- 3 tbsp. olive oil

- 2 small onions, sliced thin

- 1 tbsp. vinegar

- 1/2 C. black olives, pitted and halved

- salt and pepper

- 6 anchovy fillets, chopped

- 2 hard-boiled eggs, quartered

DIRECTIONS

Step 1

Get a large mixing bowl: Combine in it all the ingredients.

Step 2

Serve your salad right away with some pita bread.

Step 3

Enjoy.

AUNTY'S BEEF STEW

Prep Time: 20 mins

Total Time: 1 hr 35 mins

Servings per Recipe: 6

NUTRITIONAL VALUE

Calories 564.0 , Fat 27.4g , Cholesterol 50.6mg , Sodium 751.5mg , Carbohydrates 54.7g , Protein 26.6g

INGREDIENTS

- 1/4 cup olive oil

- 1 lb. stewing beef, cubed

- 1/4 tsp pepper

- 2 medium onions, chopped

- 1/2 tsp cumin

- 4 garlic cloves, crushed

- 1/2 tsp thyme

- 1/2 cup chopped cilantro leaf

- 2 cups low sodium chicken broth

- 1 hot pepper, of your choice, chopped

- salt

- 38 ounces canned chickpeas, undrained

- 1/4 cup green olives, pitted and chopped

- 4 medium tomatoes, diced

- 2 tbsps lemon juice

DIRECTIONS

Step 1

Place a stew pot over medium heat. Heat in it the oil. Brown in it the beef for 4 min.

Step 2

Stir in the hot pepper with onion, and cilantro. Cook them for 3 min.

Step 3

Stir in the garlic with a pinch of salt. Cook them for 4 min.

Step 4

Add the tomatoes with chickpeas, thyme, pepper, cumin, broth, a pinch of salt and pepper.

Step 5

Cook them until they start boiling. Put on the lid and lower the heat.

Step 6

Let them cook for 60 min. Add the lemon juice with green olives. Let them cook for an extra 6 min.

Step 7

Serve your stew warm with some bread.

Step 8

Enjoy.

EMPANADAS IN ALGERIA

Prep Time: 1 hr

Total Time: 1 hr 5 mins

Servings per Recipe: 6

NUTRITIONAL VALUE

Calories 175.4 , Fat 9.6g , Cholesterol 29.5mg , Sodium 128.8mg , Carbohydrates 12.6g , Protein 9.1g

INGREDIENTS

- 9 oz. beef mince

- 1 onion, chopped

- 1 pinch cinnamon

- 1 1/2 C. parsley, finely chopped

- 2 eggs, beaten

- 6 phyllo pastry sheets

- 6 Laughing Cow cheese wedges

- vegetable oil

DIRECTIONS

Step 1

Place a large skillet over medium heat. Heat in it a splash of oil.

Step 2

Cook in it the onion for 3 min. Stir in the beef and cook it for 5 min.

Step 3

Stir in the cinnamon, with parsley, a pinch of salt and pepper.

Step 4

Stir in the beaten eggs until they are done. Turn off the heat and let it cool down.

Step 5

Get a phyllo sheet. Put in it 2 to 3 tbsp. on one side of it. Top it with cheese.

Step 6

Pull the sheet sides to the middle then roll the sheet further over the filling tightly.

Step 7

Brush the edge with some water or beaten egg. Repeat the process with the remaining filling and sheets.

Step 8

Place a large deep skillet over medium heat. Heat in it 1.5 inches of oil.

Step 9

Cook in it the empanadas until they become golden brown. Drain them and place them on paper towels to drain.

Step 10

Serve them with a dipping sauce of your choice.

Step 11

Enjoy.

ALGERIAN CHICKEN HOT POT

Prep Time: 15 mins

Total Time: 40 mins

Servings per Recipe: 6

NUTRITIONAL VALUE

Calories 230.8 , Fat 5.1g , Cholesterol 35.0mg , Sodium 816.1mg , Carbohydrates 26.6g , Protein 19.9g

INGREDIENTS

- 3 C. chicken broth
- 2 bay leaves
- 1 chicken bouillon cube
- 1/2 tsp. dried parsley
- 2 C. cooked chicken, chopped
- salt
- 1 medium onion, chopped
- pepper
- 2 C. fresh green beans, cut
- 2 medium tomatoes, chopped
- 2 carrots, sliced
- 2 small zucchini, sliced (or 1 medium)
- 1 tsp. ground cumin
- 1 (16 oz.) cans garbanzo beans, drained
- 1 tsp. basil
- 1/4 tsp. ground red pepper
- 1 garlic clove, minced

DIRECTIONS

Step 1

Place a saucepan over medium heat. Combine in it the broth, bouillon, chopped chicken, onion, green beans, carrots, cumin, basil, garlic, bay leaves, parsley, salt, and pepper.

Step 2

Heat them until they start boiling. Lower the heat and put on the lid. Cook them for 8 to 9 min.

Step 3

Stir in the zucchini with tomatoes and cook them for 4 min.

Step 4

Stir in the red pepper with garbanzo beans. Put on the lid and heat them for 3 to 5 min.

Step 5

Adjust the seasoning of your stew then serve it.

Step 6

Enjoy.

LULU'S OVEN TAGINE

Prep Time: 30 mins

Total Time: 60 mins

Servings per Recipe: 4

NUTRITIONAL VALUE

Calories 445.4 , Fat 27.0g , Cholesterol 399.2mg , Sodium 567.3mg , Carbohydrates 27.0g , Protein 23.9g

INGREDIENTS

- 6 eggs, raw

- 2 eggs, hard-boiled, peeled and chopped

- Spices

- 1 tomatoes, deseeded and chopped

- cumin

- 1/2 onion, chopped

- turmeric

- 1-2 garlic clove, chopped

- coriander seeds

- 1 chili pepper, chopped

- harissa

- 2-3 potatoes, peeled and chopped

- salt and pepper

- 1/2 cup parsley, chopped

- Oil

- 6 ounces cheese, grated

- 2 tbsps vegetable oil

- 1 1/2 cups ground meat

DIRECTIONS

Step 1

Place a large pan over medium heat. Heat in it the oil.

Step 2

Cook in it the potatoes with turmeric, cumin, a pinch of salt and pepper for 4 min.

Step 3

Stir in the onion with meat. Cook them for 3 min. Stir in the harissa with garlic, chili pepper and a splash of water.

Step 4

Let them cook for another 3 min. Stir in the parsley with cheese, tomato, and chopped eggs then turn off the heat.

Step 5

Get a mixing bowl: Whisk in it 6 eggs with a pinch of salt and pepper.

Step 6

Add it to the potato mixture and combine them well. Spoon the mixture into a greased casserole dish.

Step 7

Sprinkle the cheese on top. Bake it for 25 to 32 min. Serve it warm.

Step 8

Enjoy.

NORTH AFRICAN DINNER BREAD

Prep Time: 1 hr 40 mins

Total Time: 2 hrs

Servings per Recipe: 1

NUTRITIONAL VALUE

Calories 88.7 , Fat 2.4g , Cholesterol 14.1mg , Sodium 83.4mg , Carbohydrates 13.9g , Protein 2.8g

INGREDIENTS

- 1/4 oz. active dry yeast

- 1/4 C. warm water, lightly salted

- 1/2 C. water

- 1 1/2 tbsp. olive oil

- 2 tbsp. sesame seeds

- 1 C. farina (cream of wheat)

- 1 egg, beaten

- 3/4 C. whole wheat flour

- cooking spray

- 1/2 tsp. salt

DIRECTIONS

Step 1

Get a mixing bowl: Combine in it the yeast with 1/4 C. of salted water.

Step 2

Place it aside and rise for 5 to 6 min.

Step 3

Get a mixing bowl: Mix in it the flour with farina and salt.

Step 4

Add the olive oil with yeast mixture and combine well. Add 1/2 C. of water and mix them well.

Step 5

Shape the mixture into a ball and cover it with a wet kitchen towel. Let it rest for 90 min.

Step 6

Before you do anything, preheat the oven to 400 F.

Step 7

Fold the sesame seeds into the dough and shape it into 15 balls.

Step 8

Place them on a greased baking sheet and coat them with the beaten egg.

Step 9

Bake them for 20 to 22 min until they become golden brown.

Step 10

Allow the rolls to cool down completely then serve them.

Step 11

Enjoy.

ORANGE BLOSSOM COOKIES

Prep Time: 10 mins

Total Time: 30 mins

Servings per Recipe: 10

NUTRITIONAL VALUE

Calories 609.4 , Fat 30.6g , Cholesterol 37.2mg , Sodium 209.8mg , Carbohydrates 78.0g , Protein 13.2g

INGREDIENTS

- 1 1/4 lbs. almonds, whole, blanched

- 1 C. sugar

- 3 C. confectioners' sugar

- 2 eggs, beaten lightly

- 2 C. water

- 1/2 C. sugar

- 1 tbsp. orange blossom water

DIRECTIONS

Step 1

To prepare the cookies:

Step 2

Before you do anything, preheat the oven to 350 F.

Step 3

Get a blender: Combine in it the sugar with almonds. pulse them several times until they become smooth.

Step 4

Transfer the mixture to mixing bowl and add to them the eggs. Stir them well until you get dough.

Step 5

Transfer the dough to working space and knead it until it becomes soft.

Step 6

Slice it into 4 pieces and transfer them to the lightly floured surface.

Step 7

Roll each quarter into a 3/4 inch rope then press it down lightly to flatten it until it becomes 1/2 inch thick.

Step 8

Slice the rope into 1-inch pieces and place them on a lined up baking sheet.

Step 9

Repeat the process with the remaining dough. Place them in the oven and cook them for 13 to 16 min.

Step 10

Once the time is up, place it aside to lose heat completely.

Step 11

To prepare the syrup:

Step 12

Place a heavy saucepan on high heat. Combine in it 1/2 C. of sugar with water.

Step 13

Heat them until they start boiling. Cook them for an extra 12 to 16 while stirring all the time.

Step 14

Turn off the heat and add the orange flower water. Let it cool down completely.

Step 15

Dip the cookies in the syrup then coat them with the powdered sugar. Serve them with some tea.

Step 16

Enjoy.

ALGERIAN SAFFRON BOWLS

Prep Time: 10 mins

Total Time: 1 hr 3 mins

Servings per Recipe: 4

NUTRITIONAL VALUE

Calories 420.5 , Fat 21.7g , Cholesterol 152.9mg , Sodium 715.0mg , Carbohydrates 6.3g , Protein 49.2g

INGREDIENTS

- 2 tbsp. olive oil
- 1 bunch cilantro, finely chopped
- 2 lbs. boneless skinless chicken breasts,
- 1 C. water
- cubed
- 8 oz. kalamata olives, pitted

- 1 tbsp. butter

- 1 lemon, juiced

- 4 garlic cloves, minced

- salt & freshly ground black pepper

- 1 tsp. saffron, crumbled

DIRECTIONS

Step 1

Place a large pot over high heat. Heat in it the oil.

Step 2

Cook in it the chicken cubes for 10 to 12 while stirring all the time.

Step 3

Add the butter, garlic, saffron, and cilantro. Cook them for 12 min while stirring often.

Step 4

Stir in the water and heat them until they start boiling.

Step 5

Lower the heat and cook them for 26 min. add the lemon juice with olives.

Step 6

Cook them for 10 min. adjust the seasoning of your stew then serve it hot with some couscous.

Step 7

Enjoy.

HOT MINTY CARROTS

Prep Time: 5 mins

Total Time: 20 mins

Servings per Recipe: 4

NUTRITIONAL VALUE

Calories 189.8 , Fat 7.7g , Cholesterol 0.0mg , Sodium 505.7mg , Carbohydrates 30.2g , Protein 3.1g

INGREDIENTS

- 2 1/2 lbs. carrots, peeled and sliced

- 1/2 tsp. hot sauce

- 1/2 tsp. sugar

- 2 tbsp. light olive oil

- 1/2 tsp. salt

- 3 garlic cloves, sliced thinly

- 2 tbsp. mint, finely chopped

- 1 lemon, juice of

- 2 tsp. cumin seeds, toasted

DIRECTIONS

Step 1

Prepare a steamer. Cook in it the carrots for 5 to 6 min until they become slightly soft.

Step 2

Place them aside along with 5 tbsp. of the steaming water.

Step 3

Place a pan over medium heat. Toast in it the cumin seeds for 1 min. Place them aside.

Step 4

Place a stew pot over medium heat. Heat in it the oil. Cook in it the carrots for 1 to 2 min.

Step 5

Stir in the steaming water with hot sauce, lemon juice, cumin seed, sugar, and salt.

Step 6

Toss them to coat. Stir in the carrots and put on half a cover.

Step 7

Let them cook 8 to 10 min until they become soft.

Step 8

Add the mint leaves and serve them right away.

Step 9

Enjoy.

BUTTERY LENTIL BOWLS

Prep Time: 20 mins

Total Time: 3 hr 20 mins

Servings per Recipe: 6

NUTRITIONAL VALUE

Calories 391.4 , Fat 15.5g , Cholesterol 58.6mg , Sodium 1096.5mg , Carbohydrates 31.7g , Protein 29.5g

INGREDIENTS

- 2 tbsp. olive oil
- 1 lb. lean lamb, cut into 1/2- 3/4 inch
- 1 carrot, scraped, and finely chopped
- cubes
- 1 garlic clove, minced
- salt, to taste

- 2 tbsp. butter

- pepper, to taste

- 1/4 tsp. cumin

- 8 C. chicken broth

- 1/4 tsp. cinnamon

- 1 C. lentils, soaked for 2 h and drained

- 1 C. orzo pasta

- 1 medium onion, minced

DIRECTIONS

Step 1

Place a pot over medium heat. Heat in it the oil.

Step 2

Brown in it the lamb pieces with a pinch of salt and pepper for 4 min.

Step 3

Stir in half of the broth and put on the lid. Cook them for 30 to 35 min until the meat becomes tender.

Step 4

Add the rest of the broth with lentils. Cook them for 16 min.

Step 5

Place a large pan over medium heat. Heat in it the butter until it melts.

Step 6

Cook in it the garlic with carrot and onion for 3 min. Transfer it to the lamb pot with orzo.

Step 7

Put on half a lid and let them cook for 10 to 12 min until the lentils and meat are done.

Step 8

Adjust the seasoning of your soup then serve it hot.

Step 9

Enjoy.

ALGERIAN WEEKEND DINNER CHICKPEAS (BEEF AND POTATOES)

Prep Time: 20 mins

Total Time: 50 mins

Servings per Recipe: 6

NUTRITIONAL VALUE

Calories 241.6 , Fat 14.8g , Cholesterol 77.3mg , Sodium 486.7mg , Carbohydrates 14.5g , Protein 12.4g

INGREDIENTS

- 1 lb. potato, peeled, boiled until tender

- 2 tbsp. butter

- 1/4 tsp. pepper

- 1 tsp. salt

- 1 medium egg, beaten

- 2 tsp. olive oil

- 2 oz. gruyere cheese, grated

- 1 small onion, finely chopped

- 1/2 lb. ground beef

DIRECTIONS

Step 1

Before you do anything, preheat the oven to 350 F.

Step 2

Get a mixing bowl: Place in it the potatoes with butter and salt.

Step 3

Mash them until they become smooth. Spread half of it in a greased casserole dish.

Step 4

Place a pan over medium heat. Heat in it the oil. Cook in it the pepper with onion and beef for 6 min.

Step 5

Drain the mixture and spread it over the potato layer.

Step 6

Cover it the with the remaining potato and spread it into an even layer.

Step 7

Pour over it the beaten eggs and top them with cheese. Bake it for 32 to 35 min until it becomes golden.

Step 8

Serve your beef casserole hot.

Step 9

Enjoy.

BAKED CHICKEN ORAN

Prep Time: 20 mins

Total Time: 2 hr

Servings per Recipe: 4

NUTRITIONAL VALUE

Calories 562.1 , Fat 43.5g , Cholesterol 183.3mg , Sodium 2767.6mg , Carbohydrates 3.3g ,
Protein 38.1g

INGREDIENTS

- 1 (3-4 lb) roasting chicken

- coarse salt

- 2 lemons, halved

- fresh ground pepper

- 2 large garlic cloves, minced

- olive oil

- 3 tbsp. unsalted butter

- 3-4 sprigs thyme

- 1 tbsp. seasoning, mixed

- 1 1/2 tbsp. coarse salt

DIRECTIONS

Step 1

Before you do anything, preheat the oven to 450 F.

Step 2

Arrange the chicken on a roasting dish. Reach under the skin to loosen it without tearing it.

Step 3

Combine the garlic with salt in a mortar. Use a pestle to mince until it becomes like a paste.

Step 4

Add the butter with spices and mix them well with your hands.

Step 5

Spread the mixture all over the chicken while reaching under the skin.

Step 6

Drizzle the lemon juice all over it then season it with some salt and pepper.

Step 7

Stuff the chicken cavity with thyme and lemon halves.

Step 8

Place it in the oven with the breast facing down. Roast it for 16 min.

Step 9

Lower the oven temperature to 350 F.

Step 10

Flip the chicken and roast it for 1 h 30 min until it becomes golden brown while basting it with some olive oil.

Step 11

Once the time is up, drain the chicken and wrap it in a piece of foil.

Step 12

Let it rest for 5 min then serve it.

Step 13

Enjoy.

BREAKFAST HONEY SEMOLINA LAYERED PASTRY

Prep Time: 5 mins

Total Time: 35 mins

Servings per Recipe: 4

NUTRITIONAL VALUE

Calories 235.1 , Fat 7.2g , Cholesterol 279.0mg , Sodium 489.2mg , Carbohydrates 29.3g , Protein 11.1g

INGREDIENTS

- 6 eggs

- 1/2 tsp. salt

- 4-5 tsp. vanilla flavoring

- 5 tbsp. self-raising flour

- 2 tbsp. fine semolina

- 1 tsp. baking powder

- Garnish

- 1/4-1/2 C. honey

DIRECTIONS

Step 1

Get a blender: Combine in it all the ingredients and blend them smooth.

Step 2

Place a small pan over low heat. Coat it with oil.

Step 3

Pour in it the batter in a circular shape and let it cook for 7 to 8 min on each side until everything rises and becomes golden.

Step 4

Cut it into 6 or 8 pieces then serve it warm with honey.

Step 5

Enjoy.

ALGERIAN SOUP POT

Prep Time: 15 mins

Total Time: 1 hr 45 mins

Servings per Recipe: 6

NUTRITIONAL VALUE

Calories 264.7 , Fat 8.5g , Cholesterol 34.6mg , Sodium 619.0mg , Carbohydrates 30.9g , Protein 16.3g

INGREDIENTS

- 1-2 tbsp olive oil

- 3-4 chicken drumsticks

- 3/4 tsp. sweet paprika

- 1 large onion, finely chopped

- 4 C. chicken stock

- 2-3 garlic cloves, minced

- 4 C. water

- 4 tsp. ras el hanout spice mix

- 17.5 oz. canned chick-peas

- 1/2 tsp. ginger

- 14 oz. chopped canned tomatoes

- 1/2 tsp. turmeric

- 1/4 preserved lemon, very finely chopped

- 1/4 tsp. cinnamon

- 1/4 C. fresh cilantro, chopped

- 1/2 lemon, juice of

DIRECTIONS

Step 1

Place a large pot over medium heat. Heat in it the oil.

Step 2

Cook in it the chicken drumsticks until they become golden brown. Drain them and place them aside.

Step 3

Stir the spices into the same pan and cook them for few seconds. Stir in back the chicken with onion, preserved lemon, garlic, stock, and water.

Step 4

Cook them until they start boiling. Lower the heat and put on the lid. Cook them for 60 min.

Step 5

Drain the chicken drumsticks, shred them and add them to the pot. Stir the chickpeas with tomato and cook them for 22 min.

Step 6

Once the time is up, add the preserved lemon with cilantro, lemon juice, and cilantro.

Step 7

Adjust the seasoning of your soup then serve hot.

Step 8

Enjoy.

ALGERIAN HONEY PUFF PASTRY

Prep Time: 2 mins

Total Time: 22 mins

Servings per Recipe: 4

NUTRITIONAL VALUE

Calories 437.3 , Fat 27.8g , Cholesterol 232.5mg , Sodium 265.5mg , Carbohydrates 40.5g , Protein 8.7g

INGREDIENTS

- 5 large eggs

- 1/4 C. sunflower oil or vegetable oil

- 1 pinch salt

- 1 tbsp. fine semolina

- 1/2-3/4 C. honey

- 2 tbsp. plain flour

- 1 1/2-2 tsp. baking powder

- 1 tsp. Vanilla flavoring or 1/2 tsp. extract

DIRECTIONS

Step 1

Get a food processor: Place in it all the ingredients and blend them smooth.

Step 2

Pour the mixture into an oil greased skillet.

Step 3

Cook it over low heat with the cover on for 15 to 16 min until it becomes puffy.

Step 4

Cover it with a plate and flip it into it. Slide it gently into the pan and put on the lid.

Step 5

Cook it for an extra 12 to 16 min until it is done.

Step 6

Drizzle over it some warm honey then serve it.

Step 7

Enjoy.

ALGERIAN SWEET LIME CAKES

Prep Time: 30 mins

Total Time: 50 mins

Servings per Recipe: 1

NUTRITIONAL VALUE

Calories 127.4 , Fat 5.0g , Cholesterol 14.1mg , Sodium 5.7mg , Carbohydrates 19.2g , Protein 2.5g

INGREDIENTS

- Cakes

- Garnish

- 3 C. ground almonds

- 2 C. of light sugar syrup

- 1 C. granulated sugar

- 2 1/2 C. icing sugar

- 4 limes, zest of, finely grated

- 3 small-medium eggs

- Roll

- 3 tbsp. corn flour

DIRECTIONS

Step 1

Before you do anything, preheat the oven to 340 F.

Step 2

Get a large mixing bowl: Mix in it the almonds with sugar, lime zest, and eggs until you get smooth dough.

Step 3

Coat a working surface with some corn flour. Place in it quarter of the mixture and shape into a log like a sausage.

Step 4

Slice into 1-inch rounds. Transfer them to a lined up baking sheet and repeat the process with the remaining dough.

Step 5

Bake them for 14 to 20 min until they become golden brown.

Step 6

Pour the syrup into a large bowl. Coat the cakes gently with the syrup then dust them with icing sugar.

Step 7

Serve them immediately.

Step 8

Enjoy.

SPICY HARISSA COUSCOUS

Prep Time: 20 mins

Total Time: 50 mins

Servings per Recipe: 6

NUTRITIONAL VALUE

Calories 805.1 , Fat 35.6g , Cholesterol 82.2mg , Sodium 564.5mg , Carbohydrates 89.1g , Protein 33.7g

INGREDIENTS

- 2 cups couscous

- 4 medium potatoes, cubed

- 1 tbsp turmeric

- 2 cups baby carrots

- 1 pinch saffron, ground

- 1 large turnip

- 1/2 tsp chili powder

- 2-3 green peppers, cored and quartered

- 1/2 tsp harissa, see appendix

- 1 (10 ounce) cans tomato paste

- 1 (15 ounces) cans chickpeas, drained

- 1/2 cup olive oil, to cover pot bottom

- 1/4 cup salted butter

- 1 large onion, chopped

- salt and pepper

- 2 whole boneless chicken breasts

- water

- 2 tbsps ras el hanout spice mix

DIRECTIONS

Step 1

Get a mixing bowl: Place in it the couscous and cover it with hot water. Place it aside.

Step 2

Place a stew pot over medium heat. Heat in it the olive oil. Cook in it the onion with a pinch of salt for 2 min.

Step 3

Stir in the chicken breasts and cook them for 3 min on each side.

Step 4

Get a small mixing bowl: Stir in it the saffron with a splash of hot water.

Step 5

Stir it into the pot with spices, a pinch of salt and pepper.

Step 6

Cover the chicken with water then cook them until they start boiling. Stir in the tomato paste with veggies.

Step 7

Stir in it the potatoes and cover the pot with a steamer.

Step 8

Stir 1/2 cup water into the soaked couscous. Pour it in the steamer and let it cook for 28 min.

Step 9

Transfer the couscous to a large serving plate. Add to it the butter with a pinch of salt.

Step 10

Mix it well with a fork. Place it aside.

Step 11

Stir the chickpeas with harissa into the veggies stew. Spoon it over the couscous then serve it hot.

Step 12

Enjoy.

SUMMER FENNEL SALAD

Prep Time: 5 mins

Total Time: 5 mins

Servings per Recipe: 4

NUTRITIONAL VALUE

Calories 169.6 , Fat 16.9g , Cholesterol 0.0mg , Sodium 31.3mg , Carbohydrates 4.3g , Protein 0.7g

INGREDIENTS

- 1 fennel bulb, sliced

- 5 tbsps olive oil

- 3 tbsps white vinegar

- salt

- pepper

DIRECTIONS

Step 1

Arrange the fennel slices on a serving plate.

Step 2

Get a mixing bowl: Whisk in it the oil with vinegar, a pinch of salt and pepper.

Step 3

Drizzle the dressing over the fennel slices. Serve it immediately.

Step 4

Enjoy.

NORTH AFRICAN EGGPLANTS

Prep Time: 20 mins

Total Time: 20 mins

Servings per Recipe: 4

NUTRITIONAL VALUE

Calories 431.6 , Fat 32.1g , Cholesterol

47.3mg , Sodium

1044.5mg , Carbohydrates

11.0g , Protein

- 25.2g

INGREDIENTS

- 1 lb. eggplant
- 1 large green bell pepper, chopped
- 1/4 cup feta cheese, crumbled
- 1 garlic clove, crushed
- crisp salad greens
- 1/2 cup olive oil
- 1/3 cup red wine vinegar
- 1 tsp dried oregano, crushed
- 1 tsp salt
- 1 (12 1/2 ounce) cans albacore tuna in
- water, drained
- 1 large tomatoes, seeded & chopped

DIRECTIONS

Step 1

Before you do anything, preheat the oven to 350 F.

Step 2

Slice the eggplants in half and place them on a baking tray.

Step 3

Coat them with olive oil and bake them for 30 min to 45 min until they become soft.

Step 4

Place them aside to cool down for few minutes. Peel them and cut them into dices.

Step 5

Get a mixing bowl: Whisk in it the garlic, oil, vinegar, oregano, and salt.

Step 6

Add the roasted eggplant dices with tomato and tuna and stir them to coat. Refrigerate it for 60 min.

Step 7

Arrange some green leaves on a serving plate. Top it with the eggplant salad.

Step 8

Garnish it with crumbled feta cheese. Serve it.

Step 9

Enjoy.

HANDMADE PASTA WITH SAUCE

Prep Time: 45 mins

Total Time: 1 hr 45 mins

Servings per Recipe: 8

NUTRITIONAL VALUE

Calories 811.6 , Fat 32.8g , Cholesterol 144.7mg , Sodium 855.1mg , Carbohydrates 79.8g , Protein 46.3g

INGREDIENTS

- Pasta

- 17.5 oz. plain flour

- 1 tbsp. sunflower oil or 1 tbsp. vegetable oil 1/2 tsp. salt

- 1 C. of tinned chickpeas

- water

- 1/4 tsp. black pepper

- corn flour, to aid rolling out

- 2 1/4 tsp. ras el hanout spice mix

- 1 tbsp. ghee

- 4 C. water

- Sauce

- 1 tsp. cinnamon

- 3 1/3 lb. chicken pieces

- 17.5 oz. long turnips, cut into 6ths

- 2 onions, finely chopped

- 9 oz. potatoes, quartered

- 1 garlic clove, minced

- 9 oz. zucchini, cut into 6ths

- 1 1/2 tsp. salt

DIRECTIONS

Step 1

To prepare the pasta:

Step 2

Get a large mixing bowl: Combine in it the flour with salt.

Step 3

Add the water gradually while mixing until you get a soft and smooth dough.

Step 4

Split the dough into 4 pieces. Sprinkle some corn flour on a working surface into a 2 mm thick circle.

Step 5

Repeat the process with the remaining dough pieces then run them through a pasta machine.

Step 6

Place them aside to dry for a few minutes. Adjust the pasta machine to make fine ribbons then run through it the dough sheets.

Step 7

Toss the noodles with some corn flour and place it aside and let it rest for 10 to 12 min.

Step 8

Drizzle over it the melted ghee and toss them to coat.

Step 9

Prepare a steamer. Place in it the noodles and cook it for 8 to 10 min until it done.

Step 10

Place a large skillet over medium heat. Heat in it the oil.

Step 11

Cook in it the chicken with garlic and onion for 10 to 12 min.

Step 12

Stir in the chickpeas with veggies, water, and spices. Cook them for 32 min over low heat with the lid on.

Step 13

Transfer the noodles to a serving plate. Top it with the chicken stew then serve it hot.

Step 14

Enjoy.

5-INGREDIENT SEMOLINA BREAD

Prep Time: 30 mins

Total Time: 50 mins

Servings per Recipe: 2

NUTRITIONAL VALUE

Calories 899.0 , Fat 22.3g , Cholesterol 0.0mg , Sodium 1167.0mg , Carbohydrates 145.6g , Protein 25.3g

INGREDIENTS

- 10.5 oz. fine semolina
- oz. medium semolina
- 3 tbsp. olive oil
- 1 tsp. salt
- 1/2 C. water

DIRECTIONS

Step 1

Get a mixing bowl: Combine in it the semolina with salt. Add the olive oil and mix them well.

Step 2

Add the water gradually while mixing until you get soft elastic dough.

Step 3

Knead it until it becomes soft. Cover it with a kitchen towel and let it rest for 32 min.

Step 4

Split the dough into 2 pieces and roll them into 1/4 inch thick disks.

Step 5

Place a grill pan over medium heat.

Step 6

Cook in it each bread loaf for 10 to 12 min on each until they become golden brown on each side.

Step 7

Serve bread warm with stew, bbq, cheese or olive oil.

Step 8

Enjoy.

HOW TO MAKE HARISSA

Prep Time: 40 mins

Total Time: 45 mins

Servings per Recipe: 8

NUTRITIONAL VALUE

Calories 73.4 , Fat 2.7g , Cholesterol 0.0mg , Sodium 451.1mg , Carbohydrates 12.5g , Protein 2.0g

INGREDIENTS

- 4.5 oz. dried hot red chili peppers, seeded
- and stemmed

- 1/2 head garlic

- 1 1/2 tsps caraway seeds

- 1 1/2 tsps ground coriander

- 1 1/2 tsps salt

- 1 tsp water

- 1-3 tbsp olive oil

DIRECTIONS

Step 1

Get a bowl: Place in it the chili peppers and cover them with hot water. Let them sit for 30 min.

Step 2

Strain them and transfer them to a food processor.

Step 3

Add the garlic with the remaining ingredients. Blend them smooth.

Step 4

Adjust the seasoning of your harissa then serve it.

Step 5

Enjoy.

SMOKED CHILI HARISSA

Prep Time: 25 mins

Total Time: 35 mins

Servings per Recipe: 1

NUTRITIONAL VALUE

Calories 1115.6 , Fat 111.4g , Cholesterol 0.0mg , Sodium 1200.5mg , Carbohydrates 32.2g , Protein 7.2g

INGREDIENTS

- 4 smoked chili peppers, seeded
- 8 dried hot red chili peppers
- 1 tbsp cumin seed
- 2 tsp coriander seeds
- 1 tsp caraway seed
- 8 garlic cloves
- 1/2 C. olive oil
- 1/2 tsp salt

DIRECTIONS

Step 1

Place the chili peppers in a bowl. Cover them with hot water. Let them sit for 25 min then drain them.

Step 2

Place a pan over medium heat. Cook in it the cumin, coriander, and caraway seeds 2 min.

Step 3

Get a food processor: Place in it the toasted seeds with chilies, garlic, olive oil, and salt.

Step 4

Process them until they become smooth. Spoon the mixture into an airtight container.

Step 5

Store it in the fridge for up to 60 days.

Step 6

Enjoy.

NORTH AFRICAN SPICE MIX

Prep Time: 10 mins

Total Time: 15 mins

Servings per Recipe: 1

NUTRITIONAL VALUE

Calories 19.1 , Fat 0.6 g , Cholesterol 0.0 mg , Sodium 583.9 mg , Carbohydrates 3.8 g , Protein 0.4 g

INGREDIENTS

- 2 tsp ground nutmeg

- 2 tsp ground coriander

- 1 tsp cayenne pepper

- 2 tsp ground cumin

- 1 tsp cardamom powder

- 2 tsp ground ginger

- 1 tsp ground allspice

- 2 tsp turmeric

- 1/2 tsp ground cloves

- 2 tsp salt

- 2 tsp cinnamon

- 1 1/2 tsp sugar

- 1 1/2 tsp paprika

- 1 1/2 tsp ground black pepper

DIRECTIONS

Step 1

In a bowl, add all the ingredients and mix well.

Step 2

Transfer the mixture into a glass jar and seal tightly.

Step 3

Store in a cool, dry place.

CARROT AND CELERY SOUP

Prep Time: 5 mins

Total Time: 40 mins

Servings per Recipe: 3

NUTRITIONAL VALUE

Calories 250.0 , Fat 1.3g , Cholesterol 0.0mg , Sodium 62.4mg , Carbohydrates 46.6g , Protein 15.5g

INGREDIENTS

- 1 onion, finely chopped

- 1 tsp. ground cumin

- 2 carrots, finely chopped

- 1 tsp. ground coriander

- 2 sticks celery, finely chopped

- 5 oz. green lentils

- 3 garlic cloves, crushed

- 2 pints vegetable stock

- 3 tomatoes, chopped

- 1 lemon

- 1/2 tsp. turmeric

- 1 bunch coriander, chopped

DIRECTIONS

Step 1

Place a large skillet over medium heat. Heat in it the oil.

Step 2

Cook in it the onion, carrots, and celery for 3 min. Stir in the garlic with tomato, and seasonings.

Step 3

Cook them for 2 to 3 min. Stir in the lentil, stock, salt, and pepper.

Step 4

Put on the lid and lower the heat. Cook them for 35 min.

Step 5

Once the time is up, stir in the coriander with lemon juice. Serve it hot.

Step 6

Enjoy.

DOLMAS BISKRA

Prep Time: 50 mins

Total Time: 1 hr 35 mins

Servings per Recipe: 1

NUTRITIONAL VALUE

Calories 30.0 , Fat 0.5g , Cholesterol 0.0mg , Sodium 138.5mg , Carbohydrates 5.7g , Protein 0.7g

INGREDIENTS

- Insides

- 50 grape leaves

- 4 tbsp. water

- 1 large red pepper, diced

- salt and black pepper

- 1 large red vine-ripened tomatoes, diced

- Sauce

- 1/2 large onion, diced

- 1/2 large onion, diced

- 4 garlic cloves, minced

- 1 large vine-ripened tomatoes, diced

- 1 1/2 C. basmati rice or 1 1/2 C. long grain 2 garlic cloves, minced

- rice

- 1/2 tsp. cinnamon

- 1 tsp. paprika

- 1 chicken stock cube

- 1/2 tsp. cinnamon

- 4 C. water

- 1/2 tsp. ras el hanout spice mix

- 1 tsp. lemons or 1 tsp. lime juice

- 1 tbsp. olive oil

- salt and black pepper

DIRECTIONS

Step 1

To prepare the leaves:

Step 2

Bring a large salted pot of water to a boil.

Step 3

Trim and wash the leaves then cook them in the hot water for 16 min.

Step 4

Drain them and place them aside.

Step 5

To prepare the filling:

Step 6

Place a large pan over medium heat. Heat in it some olive oil.

Step 7

Add to it the peppers with tomato and onion. Cook them for 3 min.

Step 8

Stir in the garlic and cook them for 3 to 4 min. Stir in the spices and cook them for 1 min.

Step 9

Once the time is up, turn off the heat and add the water with remaining olive oil and rice.

Step 10

Place the filling aside to cool down.

Step 11

To prepare the broth:

Step 12

Place a large pot over medium heat. Heat in it the olive oil. Cook in it the tomato with onion for 3 min.

Step 13

Stir in the spices with the stock cube, water, and lemon juice. Cook them for 16 min.

Step 14

Once the time is up, turn off the heat and strain the broth.

Step 15

Place a leaf on a plate. Put in it 1 tsp. of the filling.

Step 16

Pull the sides over the filling then roll it forward like a cigar.

Step 17

Repeat the process with the remaining ingredients.

Step 18

Arrange the stuffed leaves in a pot then place on top of them a plate.

Step 19

Pour the hot broth on top then put on the lid. Let them cook for 26 min over low heat.

Step 20

Serve your stuffed leaves hot.

Step 21

Enjoy.

ORANGE HONEY BEIGNETS (DOUGHNUTS)

Prep Time: 60 mins

Total Time: 1 hr 15 mins

Servings per Recipe: 12

NUTRITIONAL VALUE

Calories 548.4 , Fat 37.7g , Cholesterol 46.5mg , Sodium 49.8mg , Carbohydrates 50.8g , Protein 3.9g

INGREDIENTS

- 3 eggs
- 1/4 cup olive oil
- 3 tbsps lemon juice
- 1/4 cup orange juice
- 1 1/4 cups sugar
- 1 large orange, peel
- 1/3 cup creamed honey
- 1/4 cup sugar
- 2 cups oil
- 2 cups all-purpose flour
- 1 tsp baking powder
- 1 1/4 cups cold water

DIRECTIONS

Step 1

To prepare the dough:

Step 2

Get a mixing bowl: Whisk in it the eggs, oil, orange juice, 1 tsp orange peel and sugar.

Step 3

Add the baking powder with flour and a pinch of salt. Combine them until you get a smooth dough.

Step 4

Transfer it to a greased bowl. Put on the lid and let the batter sit for 46 min.

Step 5

To prepare the syrup:

Step 6

Place a saucepan over medium heat. Stir in it the water, lemon juice, and sugar.

Step 7

Cook them until they start boiling. Lower the heat and let them cook for 6 min.

Step 8

Stir in the honey and cook them for extra 6 min.

Step 9

To prepare the donuts:

Step 10

Shape the dough into 12 balls. Flatten each one of them into a 3 inches circle.

Step 11

Make a 1 1/2 inch hole in the center of each dough circle.

Step 12

Place a deep pan over medium heat. Heat in it the oil.

Step 13

Fry in it the donuts for 2 to 3 min on each side until they become golden brown.

Step 14

Garnish your donuts with some icing sugar then serve them.

Step 15

Enjoy.

AFRICAN TUNA SANDWICHES WITH HAND MADE BREAD

Prep Time: 2 hr

Total Time: 3 hr

Servings per Recipe: 4

NUTRITIONAL VALUE

Calories 948.8 , Fat 30.5g , Cholesterol 196.5mg , Sodium 1516.7mg , Carbohydrates 138.6g , Protein 31.4g

INGREDIENTS

- Sauce

- 2 tbsps oil

- 500 g pumpkin

- 1 tsp salt

- 4 garlic cloves, mashed

- 1 egg

- 1/4 tsp cayenne pepper

- 1 1/4 cups water

- 1/4 tsp paprika

- Filling

- 1/4 cup oil

- 3 potatoes, boiled cubed

- 1 tsp caraway seed, ground

- 4 eggs, hardboiled, sliced

- 1 lemon, juice

- 4 pickles, sliced lengthwise

- Buns

- 3.5 oz. olives, pitted

- 4 cups flour

- 3.5 oz. canned tuna, drained

- 2 tsps yeast

DIRECTIONS

Step 1

To prepare the pumpkin sauce:

Step 2

Place a pan over medium heat. Heat in it the oil. Stir in it the garlic with pumpkin for 7 min.

Step 3

Stir in the cayenne pepper with caraway seeds, 1 cup of water, a pinch of salt and lemon juice. Cook them until they become soft.

Step 4

Mash them until they become smooth. Place it aside.

Step 5

To prepare the buns:

Step 6

Get a mixing bowl: Mix in it all the dough ingredients until you get a smooth dough.

Step 7

Transfer it to a floured surface and knead it for 5 min. Divide it into 20 balls.

Step 8

Place them on greased baking trays then cover them with a kitchen towel. Let them rest for 45 min.

Step 9

Place a deep pan over medium heat. Heat in it 2 inches of oil. Deep fry in it the dough ball until they become golden brown.

Step 10

Drain the bread rolls and place them on paper towels to drain.

Step 11

To prepare the filling:

Step 12

Get a mixing bowl: Stir in it the eggs with pickles, olives, tuna, potatoes, a pinch of salt and pepper.

Step 13

Slice the bread rolls in half. Spread the pumpkin sauce in the bottom halves. Top them with the tuna mixture.

Step 14

Cover them with the top halves. Serve your sandwiches immediately.

Step 15

Enjoy.

CHILI SAUSAGE AND POTATO STEW

Prep Time: 5 mins

Total Time: 1 hr 15 mins

Servings per Recipe: 4

NUTRITIONAL VALUE

Calories 374.9 , Fat 17.8g , Cholesterol 279.0mg , Sodium 152.7mg , Carbohydrates 40.5g , Protein 14.4g

INGREDIENTS

- 3-4 tbsps olive oil

- 4 medium potatoes, cubed

- 6 small spicy sausage, sliced

- 1-2 tbsp tomato paste

- 6 eggs

- 1-4 tsp harissa

- salt

- 3-4 garlic cloves, skinned and crushed

- 2-3 dried chilies, seeded and chopped

- 2 tsps crushed caraway seeds

- 2 tsps paprika

DIRECTIONS

Step 1

Place skillet over medium heat. Heat in it the oil.

Step 2

Cook in it the potatoes for 3 min. Stir in the tomato paste with harissa, garlic, caraway seeds and paprika.

Step 3

Season them with a pinch of salt. Add enough water to cover the potatoes.

Step 4

Put on the lid and let them cook for 45 min over low heat. Stir in the sausages and let them cook for 16 min.

Step 5

Get a mixing bowl: Whisk in it the eggs with a pinch of salt and pepper.

Step 6

Add it to the stew and mix them well. Let them cook until the eggs are done.

Step 7

Adjust the seasoning of your stew then serve it warm with some bread.

Step 8

Enjoy.

HOW TO MAKE BAKLAVA (LAYERED HONEY PASTRY DESSERT)

Prep Time: 1 hr

Total Time: 2 hr 10 mins

Servings per Recipe: 20

NUTRITIONAL VALUE

Calories 545.7 , Fat 36.0g , Cholesterol 35.6mg , Sodium 231.2mg , Carbohydrates 51.3g , Protein 8.0g

INGREDIENTS

- Dough

- 1/4 tsp. ground cinnamon

- 24 oz. plain flour

- 1 tsp. vanilla sugar

- 1 1/8 C. water

- 2 tsp. melted ghee

- 1 C. melted ghee mixed with sunflower oil

- 5 oz. orange blossom water

- or vegetable oil

- Syrup

- 1/2 tsp. salt

- 2 1/2 C. honey

- 18 oz. chopped nuts, use almonds, walnuts, 1 1/4 C. orange flower water pecans

- Optional

- 4.5 oz. granulated sugar

- 1 1/4 C. extra of melted ghee (clarified butter)

DIRECTIONS

Step 1

To prepare the dough:

Step 2

Get a mixing bowl: Combine in it the flour with salt and oil. Mix them well.

Step 3

Mix in the water until you get a smooth dough. Divide it in half.

Step 4

Shape one half into gold size balls and place them on a baking tray. Cover them with a kitchen towel.

Step 5

Place the other half of the dough aside and cover it as well.

Step 6

Run a dough ball through a pasta machine to form it into a sausage shape.

Step 7

Place it on a corn flour dusted working surface and roll it until it becomes 4 mm thick sheet.

Step 8

Heat the ghee until it melts and brushes a baking sheet with some of it.

Step 9

Lay in it the dough sheet and coat the top of it with some ghee.

Step 10

Repeat the process with the remaining dough to make 5 more sheets.

Step 11

Arrange them on top of the first sheets in a crisscross shape.

Step 12

To prepare the filling:

Step 13

Get a food processor: Combine in it the nuts. Pulse them several times until they become finely chopped.

Step 14

Transfer it to a mixing bowl and add to it the sugar, cinnamon, vanilla powder and orange blossom water. Mix them well.

Step 15

Repeat the process with the remaining dough while laying the sheets over the filling in a crisscross shape and coating them with ghee.

Step 16

Use a sharp knife to cut into diamonds then press a nut into each diamond.

Step 17

Coat it with the remaining ghee then bake it for 60 to 70 min.

Step 18

To prepare the syrup:

Step 19

Place a heavy saucepan over high heat. Heat in it the honey with orange blossom water.

Step 20

Pour it while hot all over the baklava then let it sit for 10 to 15 min.

Step 21

Cut it through again then serve it with some tea.

Step 22

Enjoy.

www.ingramcontent.com/pod-product-compliance
Lightning Source LLC
Chambersburg PA
CBHW080904160726
48000CB00009B/2849